# Fireplace & Mantel Ideas

by John Lewman

FOX BOOKS
Fox Chapel Publishing Co Inc.

1970 Broad Street
East Petersburg, PA 17520

We gratefully thank the following for permission to reprint materials and reproduce photographs:

Superior Clay Corporation/ Uhrichsville, Ohio

Heat-N-Glo/ Minneapolis, MN

Stone Magic/ Dallas, TX

Brickstone Studios/ Lincoln, NE

Superior Fireplace/ Fullerton, CA

Wohners Inc./ Englewood, NJ

Wally Little/ Las Vegas, NV

Journal of Light Construction

To order your copy of this book please send check or money order for cover price plus $3.50 to:
Fox Chapel Book Orders
1970 Broad Street
East Petersburg, PA 17520
*Try your favorite local or mail-order book supplier first!*
Printed in China

# Acknowledgements

My personal thanks and hats off goes first to Alan Giagnocavo, publisher, whose foresight, patience and encouragement made this book possible. Without his support it would never have seen the light of day.

My heartfelt thanks to my beautiful wife Cynthia for teaching me Pagemaker, and for her many hours of professional coaching.

Special thanks go to John Wohner of Wohner's Incorporated. John freely shared the fascinating written and photo history of his outstanding almost 100 year old family firm.

Peggy Jones of Fireside Magic willingly shared her graphics files spending many hours researching and compiling wonderfully useful materials.

And a very special thanks to Wally and Terry Little for sharing their original designs and work history.

In addition, a hearty thanks to Jim Buckley for his excellent Rumford Fireplace data.

All of you have been totally supportive and cooperative and have contributed greatly to the success of the **Fireplace & Mantel Ideas** book. You have made authoring this work a real pleasure.

# Introduction

Our basic human need for light, warmth and security has developed in us an enduring love and a passion for fire. Over thousands of years and millions of experiments we have conquered the use of fire and made it the centerpiece and focus of our homes.

The fireplace and mantel are now the center of our social interaction, food preparation and comfort. And all of us find gathering around the fireplace to be the warmest and friendliest place to share our lives and experiences with friends and family.

Planning the place and function of your fireplace is one of the great joys of designing your living space. Based on today's environmental needs, you'll want to begin with designing for an efficient, heat-circulating firebox.

The period style and decor of your home is the next consideration. Calculating available space, the size and shape of the room the fireplace resides in, and the tastes and needs of family members also play an important role in your final decisions.

Expressing your individual style is easy with today's wide variety of fireplace mantels and surrounds. You can begin your interior planning with the mantel. Choosing a dramatic design can dictate your style, emphasize a theme, or add an element of interest and surprise to the interior of any room.

Ranging in price from moderate to exotic, the mantels shown in the **Fireplace & Mantel Ideas** book will inspire your creative efforts and provide both design details and sources for the mantel of your dreams.

We hope you enjoy the designs as much as we enjoyed creating and compiling them, and wish you the best in your endeavors as you explore the many possibilities available to you in this fascinating and worthwhile book.

John Lewman

# Table of Contents

*Brickstone Cast-Stone Mantel*

# Chapter One

# The Living Fireplace

## A Brief History of the Hearth

**Today you can easily realize your dream of enjoying a colorful, heartwarming fire while surrounded by a classically stylish and beautiful mantel.**

The fireplace acts as the center gathering place of a home and holds a permanent place of comfort in all of our hearts. With today's new technologies your

*High quality fireplace inserts for wall or corner installations are available from a variety of vendors (Heat-N-Glo).*

options are plentiful. You can easily build your own fireplace and mantel or install one of hundreds of quality, made-to-order packages that will create a delightful focus in any room or space.

In the history of the fireplace, there has never existed such an exciting variety of designs, fuels and installation choices as exists in today's expanding market. You are going to enjoy discovering the wealth of strikingly beautiful, and at the same time easily serviceable, products and methods that when combined make up today's vast offering of home hearth options.

For all of us who enjoy the convenience of the TV remote control, there now exists a tremendous variety of automatic fireplaces that light beautifully with a click of the finger. You'll bask in the instantly enjoyable warmth of gas-fueled golden fires that can be lit while you lie

comfortably under your bed covers on a chilly morning. The new remote-controlled gas-fired inserts burn as beautifully as any wood-fired fireplace and are completely safe and dependable.

You'll find that many of the gas-fired units will vent through any wall, without the expense and high maintenance of a brick chimney. Other more advanced gas units require no venting at all and consume all the gas fuel safely without any perceptible fumes or after-odors.

*Superior vent-free inserts provide many options.*

For the dedicated fireplace enthusiast who requires the tradition and realism of a "real" wood fireplace, we've included the details for building the famous, high efficiency

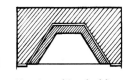

*Top view of Rumford fire-box showing angled sides, shallow depth and back.*

*The Rumford fire-box straight back.*

Rumford-style fireplace using Superior Clay's lifetime ceramic fireplace kits. The kits are expertly manufactured.

*This striking design incorporates a high-tech woodburning insert. The mantel and surround are dramatically executed in quality ceramic tiles. A variety of themes are possible using this technique and allow for a striking design that can be built into almost any decor (Heat-N-Glo).*

In **Fireplace & Mantel Ideas** you will find that whatever style of decor you choose as a theme, we've included ideas and the technology to help you realize your vision with spectacular flair and serviceability. Factory-built fireplaces can be inserted into any wall, then framed with a mantel that complements the room's decor. A gas fireplace can be positioned in the center of the

*This classic woodburning fireplace is complemented by a beautifully designed and high quality cast stone mantel (Stone Magic).*

The Rumford design is extremely efficient and provides superior design opportunities.

Also included are the new clean burn woodburning appliances that

*Woodburning inserts come in a wide variety of current styles.*

offer virtually smoke-free and dramatically higher efficiencies than the standard inserts that were constructed using the old technologies. All this simply adds up to an amazing increase in comfort, convenience, and very real fuel savings from every load of fuel you purchase.

We feel the best news of all is from the freedom of design when using the gas-fired units that are easily vented through any wall. No longer is the fireplace limited to the living or family room. Fireplaces can be easily designed to work well in the kitchen, bedroom, bath, library, den or office. The fireplace can be freestanding, under a window, or in a corner while fitting precisely into your design decor of choice.

*A dancing fire adds charm and warmth to any gathering of family and friends. With today's modern fireplace conveniences, maintaining a healthy fire is easy, and servicing and cleanup are minimized.*

kitchen and framed with a simple easy-maintenance tile motif. A quiet bedroom space can be enhanced dramatically with the warmth and beauty of a freestanding ventless island fireplace. An unused corner can become a striking focal point in an otherwise ordinary room. Imagine the comfort of bathing in a bathroom that is lighted and warmed by the glow of a gentle fire. Beautiful mantel designs are available in the refined tradition of each historical era. Every theme is centered around celebrating the joy of the open fire.

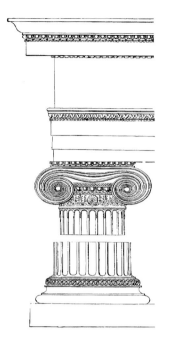

From Colonial to Contemporary, the fireplace is a pleasurable addition to the ambiance of any living space. Creating your own special fireplace hearth complete with the latest technological advances is completely possible. Come with us now as we help you discover the new joys of the hearth. Whether planning to build your own fireplace and mantel, or having it all installed by a professional, you'll find the journey enjoyable and enlightening.

### The Classical World: Greece and Rome, 60 A.D.

The exciting art of fireplace mantel design extends back in time to the illustrious classical world of Greece and Rome. Our modern culture draws heavily from the influence of these masters of aesthetics and construction.

An important and influential feature of Greek and Roman design was the close connection

*This early Roman living area demonstrates the classical forms and proportions of the era.*

between decorating themes and their everyday lives. Religion, sports, business and pleasure were all captured in beautiful designs rendered in mosaics, tile, plaster and stone. They added decorative themes to mantels, walls and

*Greek and Roman craftsmen were masters of the decorated column.*

floors. Colored marble, stone and tile were adhered to columns and overlays, creating dramatic fireplaces that from the earliest times were the heart and soul of every family gathering and celebration.

From the smallest hut to the expanding villas, the ancient classical craftsmen carefully constructed the joyful interface between man and fire. Their celebration of living is so primal that we still long to feel the joy of fire in our own homes to this day. Beautiful themes from these early times are part of our shared architectural history.

### Byzantine, 900 A.D.

The Byzantine era speaks of unrivaled luxury, refinement and bold sophistication. The Byzantine period is the link between ancient Rome and the Middle Ages and

*The Byzantine period designs are elaborate and dramatic and include Greek, Roman and Papal themes. This beautiful surround is in the living area of a rich merchant's palace.*

was centered in Constantinople, where the lavish traditions of both the Greek and Roman world mingled with the opulence of the Orient.

Rooms were paneled with exotic woods and heated with magnificent brick and stone fireplaces. Gold and silver work abounded, as did green marble and red sandstone. Cast bronze enhanced designs and added the warm glow of exotic metals.

The overwhelming and dramatic fireplace became a common theme in palaces and villas. Great detail was added with fluted columns, elaborate carvings and beautiful sculptures.

Private homes enjoyed elegantly designed mantels that were the center of domestic activities and the focal point for study, reflection and rest.

Tapestries, wall hangings and oil paintings became common among the well-to-do and were often incorporated with the

*The Medieval house was a dynamically active environment that centered around the hearth. The master and his mistress and children happily conversed with servants and visitors in colorful surroundings that were extremely functional and ruggedly constructed.*

*This dramatic modern design in cast stone captures the regal and aggressive emotions of the early Greek and Roman statuary. Modern cast stone mantels capture the latest features of the new technologies and are quick and easy to install (Stone Magic).*

fireplace as the central point of interest in a room.

***Medieval, 1300 A.D.*** Great houses during the Medieval period were bright, and full of life and color. There existed an obvious lack of self-conscious planning. Designs were robust and full of vigor and strength. Heavy woods, striking geometric patterns and simplistic carvings reflected the themes of everyday living. The fireplace remained the focal point of all activities of the home.

***The Renaissance, 1500 A.D.*** Opulently rich with the magnificent works of Leonardo da Vinci, along with Michelangelo, Bramante and Raphael, the Renaissance established Italy as a world design center. Many of the most beautiful and important themes of interior design were developed in this astounding era. The fireplace maintained importance in interior design with the chimney piece as the most pronounced element.

Sumptuous mantels, tapestries, paintings, sculpture and furniture flourished in country villas and suburban palaces. Mantels were heavily architectural, reflecting ancient Greek and Roman columns, capitals and sculpture. Designs were often

*The new prosperity of the merchant classes are reflected here in this magnificent living area heavily embellished with carved wood and ornament.*

executed in magnificent proportions. Designs varied from the dark-minded and bizarre to the lighthearted and playful. All were executed with great detail and complexity.

***The Age of the Baroque, 1600 A.D.*** The seventeenth century was the beginning of modern concepts in interior design

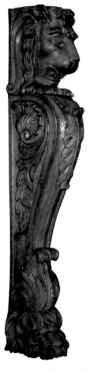

*This modern luxuriously carved leg reflects the tastes and styles of the Renaissance Era. A master craftsman of the Wohner family carved this masterpiece by hand for a mantel created for a prominent U.S. customer. The Renaissance Era is a rich source of design ideas that is regularly tapped by today's artists and craftsmen. During this period, the ruling and moneyed classes experienced a burst of personal freedom as old shackles of religion, poverty and ignorance gave way. Today's museums are replete with outstanding examples of Renaissance art and craftsmanship. The society's new consciousness of its place in the universe was expanded by the emerging sciences. These discoveries went hand-in-hand with the rediscovery of the classical civilizations. The greatest designers of all time are from this era. Men like Leonardo da Vinci, Michelangelo, Bramante and Raphael each left us a priceless legacy of masterfully aesthetic and beautifully emotional craftsmanship.*

and furnishings. The theme of the Baroque interior was to create a magnificent background for social events. Furnishings and decor began to reflect social status and stability. Each element of the room was designed to work with all the other elements to obtain an overall harmony of design. The fireplace became even more reinforced as the center of life in an active room.

The grandly designed themes of the era were a combination of Classical Roman and Papal (Catholic) origin. The chimney piece of the Renaissance protruded too much into the social scenes of the Baroque society, and began to recede. After plasterwork, the most characteristic medium was sculpting and wood carving, which reached unequalled perfection in the English designs for estates and villas crafted by Grinling Gibbons. Fireplace mantels were designed and executed as magnificently carved surrounds, very

*The Great Houses of the Baroque period were decorated with beautifully detailed oak panels surrounding an elaborate and overwhelming mantel. Many of the designs include naturalistic motifs such as massively carved fruit, swelling curves and elaborate furnishings and tapestries.*

similar to what is found in many late nineteenth century and today's modern homes.

***The Rococo Style, 1700 A.D.*** is the last original expression of

*The Wohner family designed and built this hand-carved example of a Renaissance fireplace and surround. The woodburning firebox includes optional glass doors and fireproof steel sliding screens operated by a drawstring.*

the aristocratic ideal in European art. Its sources are complex, and both the Italians and French claim to be its creators. Its first appearance in interior design was definitely in France. Naturalistic designs in the form of seashell motifs and arabesques are plentiful in these overtly expressive and magnificently carved compositions.

Berain produced many engravings for chimney pieces that consisted of an elaborate over-mantel with a large central clock flanked by porcelain vases. Large over-mantel mirrors often faced each other across the room. This theme has remained a design element in aristocratic homes to this day.

The overall theme of Rococo is to create a feeling of extreme luxury. This can be achieved with elegant materials and elaborate

*Rococo period mantels and surrounds were highly imaginative, if sometimes grotesque. Nature and human themes were woven into overwhelming statements that were intended to deeply impress. This sketch by an unknown artist of the era is a fine example of the exaggerated Rococo styling features.*

A classical Rococo style mantel designed and hand carved by the Wohner Company. Note the careful balance of curve and line, and the extreme care taken in creating a dynamic and exciting surround.

design, or by a mixture of standard materials and skillfully applied colors in the form of gilded paints, textures and carved or stamped period appliques.

***Neoclassicism, 1880 A.D.***
This era encompasses a wide variety of styles and includes some of the most elegant designs of Europe and America.

The Empire style competed with Regency, Biedermeier and Victorian to be considered the most "chic" interior design statement of the times. All the Neoclassical themes were aimed at imitating the styles of art found in the Ancient World. This emphasis created international themes that were popular in all of

Europe and in the Americas.

The American versions of Neoclassicism were developed incorporating ornate lines embellished with ornately carved woods, overlays of gilt, brass and ormolu. With Yankee precision the American craftsmen shaped their timeless designs avoiding the excessive opulence of the old European masters.

Many of the Neoclassical styles are popular yet today and are found in many different types

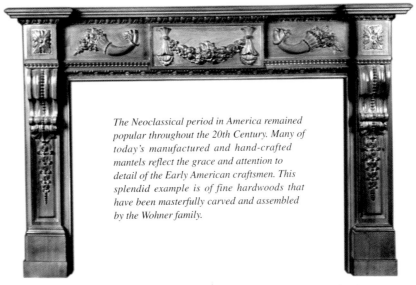

*The Neoclassical period in America remained popular throughout the 20th Century. Many of today's manufactured and hand-crafted mantels reflect the grace and attention to detail of the Early American craftsmen. This splendid example is of fine hardwoods that have been masterfully carved and assembled by the Wohner family.*

*This unusual example of the Neoclassical style has an interesting and useful side chamber.*

and sizes of homes in both Europe and America. The craftsmen of the late twentieth century especially favor the clean yet opulent presentations.

***Arts and Crafts Movement, 1880 A.D.*** William Morris was resistant to mass production. He believed in remaining true to the materials at hand, and to the honesty of timeless design. The

movement was popular in America and was termed the "Craftsman Style." The designs were simple, popular themes, and sometimes included elaborate cutout motifs such as hearts or spears. Other motifs were inspired by nature. The later works of this

*Both English and American homes enjoyed the delicate rendition of the Neoclassical period. The mantels were often a beautiful balance of brick and hand-carved and stained hardwoods.*

*A fine example of the overly ornate Arts and Crafts style mantels. Note the floral details.*

period were the inspirational base of the dramatic Art Nouveau style.

***Art Nouveau Period.*** In 1890 A.D., Europe developed its own version of the sinuous Art Nouveau style. Designs were shaped in a molten style. Many items had not even one straight line in them. Growing plant forms

*This Art Nouveau classic is constructed of cast plaster. The dramatic curves and details are typical of the times.*

abound. The German approach tended to be angular with stylized rose flower themes.

***Art Deco, 1920 A.D.*** The Art Deco style dominated fashionable circles in the '20s and '30s. Luxurious and opulent, the look focused on leather, glass, lacquer, chrome and ivory. The forms tended to be sleek and stream-lined and were based on geometric shapes and motifs. Sunrises, trees, flowers, and animal forms exist in architectural stylizations that add emotion and texture to the themes.

***Designing your own unique fireplace.*** This rich heritage of design from the various stylistic periods provides an excellent reference for contemplating the right mantel for your particular needs. Any of the period designs can be applied as a focal point in just about any room or home.

If you are designing using a simple, modern theme, adding a baroque or Art Deco mantel may be just the ticket for adding excitement and focus to your creation. On the other hand, a sleek and stylized mantel can create a quiet elegance in an otherwise opulent and luxurious setting. Consider using alternate materials and methods that are

*The classic Art Deco period included designs executed in plain and exotic metals. This masterpiece is of burnished bronze and chrome.*

adaptations of the themes and popular colors of the present interior design motifs. There are many possibilities. The choice is yours!

---

***Right page: Late 20th Century Neoclassical***

 This current rendition of the famous Neoclassical style is easily executed and economical to build with common tools. The base material is high density particle board which provides a stone-hard and smooth surface for enamels or lacquers so prevalent during the era.

 The individual components that make up the columns are simple shapes sawn on a table saw with edges rounded with a router or sander. The material is basic three-quarter inch thick stock available from most lumber yards. The bases of the columns have a sculptured look created by the addition of blocks stack-glued to give the variety of dimensions shown. The fireplace insert is an all-steel rear-vent unit. This particular style has the popular arch top. The classical design can be finished with a variety of techniques and color combinations true to the era. It can be built as a standard mantel height or with the ceiling extension as shown. This design wears well with almost any style of interior decor. (Crest by Brickstone.)

*Heat-N-Glo Fireplace Products*

# Chapter Two

# Fireplace Technology

## Hearth Size, Location and Chimney Construction

**With today's high-efficiency and cost-effective designs, heating with a living fire makes aesthetic and financial sense.**

**Heating with living fire appliances makes a lot of sense.**

If you are like many of us today, much of your living is enjoyed in mainly one or two rooms of your house or apartment. A great advantage of the new fire technologies is the "heat-zoning" possibilities when using wall-mounted or freestanding appliances. These heating units are perfect for

*This modern kitchen enjoys an increase in efficiency and space utilization with a wraparound presentation (Superior).*

zoning the heat of your home, allowing you to concentrate comfortable air temperatures in the rooms that are used the most.

A big plus of the new units is their high efficiency. Many are more efficient than the standard home forced-air gas furnaces, and

*Superior developed this amazing freestanding fireplace that is completely vent free. These amazing units can be placed just about anywhere in the home.*

are ideal for supplementing your heating needs while at the same time lowering your heating fuel bills.

You can easily keep unused rooms at dollar-saving cooler

*The standard forced air gas furnace loses 25% of developed heat through the walls of the metal duct work. Insulating of the ducts does help, but duct work passing through inner walls is not accessible.*

temperatures, while in the main socializing areas you, your family and guests are basking in the glow of a natural fire.

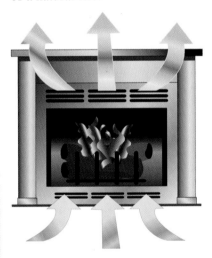

*High efficiency inserts draw cool air off the floor and expel warm air from louvers positioned at the top edge of the firebox. Efficiencies can be as high as 80% to 90%.*

The new technology gas and wood fireplace inserts are actually more refined and economical to operate than all but the most advanced modern gas furnaces.

A gas furnace system will sometimes lose a percentage of its heat through the surfaces of the ducting that runs from the furnace

*Left Page: The magnificent ocean view is enhanced with the addition of a traditional mantel surrounding a Heat-N-Glo rear-vented gas insert. The insert is chimney-free and allows for the dramatic arched window that is aesthetically positioned over the mantel. Rear-vented inserts are available in both wood- and gas-burning models from a variety of quality manufacturers. Many of the units are EPA-approved and are high-efficiency models that rival the best furnaces in heat output.*

The real beauty of today's new fire appliances is the incredible array of high efficiency installations that are possible.

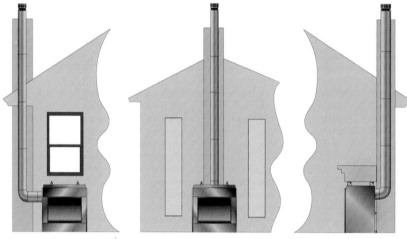

*Companies like Heat-N-Glo and Superior provide a selection of venting arrangements for their fire appliances. Gas appliances are usually the easiest to place in a floor plan and allow for top, rear, left and right side positioning.*

decks and patios can all benefit from the installation of a real fire appliance.

If you are considering the cost of a real fire appliance in comparison to the resale value of your

*Your creativity has no limits with the new technology. Corner designs can be executed in a number of stylish and successful executions. Your fireplace can truly be tailored to fit your needs.*

through the inner walls to various rooms of the house. The actual amount of heat from the registers will be reduced by up to 25 percent.

In contrast, the inserts on the market today have actual efficiency ratings of 80 to 90 percent. A big portion of the efficiency is due to the fact that there is no heat loss through ducting. The heat from the fuel burned is concentrated fully in the room

*Dramatic styling beautifies this unusual fireplace. The all-steel insert allows for a safe and low-cost installation (Superior).*

containing the hearth appliance.

In any situation you can depend on fully heating a single room. In many situations, two or more rooms can be heated if careful planning is employed.

The real beauty of the new appliances is the incredible variety of installations that are possible. Manufacturers have created beautiful fire appliances for any room in the house. Bathrooms, bedrooms, living and family rooms, kitchens, dens, home offices, basement areas, garages, even outdoor entertainment areas such as

home, you'll usually find that each added appliance will increase your home's value far beyond the cost of installation.

*Brickstone Studios designed and built this magnificent cast stone fireplace mantel and relief mural. The design fits perfectly with the Corinthian theme of the decor. Brickstone mantels are well engineered and are of extremely high quality for generations of enjoyment.*

And in addition to being a great investment, you'll daily enjoy relaxing in the glow and warmth of a living fire. What's more, you can design the installation of your dreams drawing from the incredible array of fireboxes and surrounds to create a dramatic focus to the family's favorite living spaces in your home.

**How to calculate the correct output and dimensions for your fireplace:**

*Size:* Choosing the size of your heat-producing appliance is critical to the success of your installation. If the heat output is too great, the room will become uncomfortably warm. In contrast, if the heat output is inadequate to warm the room to a pleasant temperature, the unit could run constantly, causing a sizeable increase in your fuel bills.

***Economical Steel Wood-Burning Fireplace.** In today's home building environment, cost is always an issue. The Superior KR models 38-3 and 43 offer homeowners the warmth and charm of a beautiful fireplace at the lowest possible cost. The clean-face design features no exposed grills. Surround materials can be installed right up to the front opening, giving the look of a traditional masonry fireplace.*

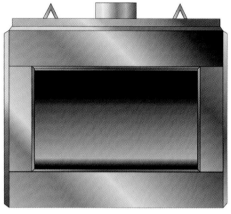

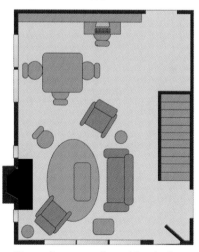

*The KR-38-3 has a 38" screen opening. Both use a space saving chimney design system. Options include an outside combustion air kit and a choice of decorator doors in a variety of style and colors.*

The Environmental Protection Agency has certified many of the new appliances. The certification includes efficiency and safety specifications. We advise that you install EPA-approved appliances exclusively.

Other things to consider when planning for efficiency are your

***Side Note:** Stored wood must be kept covered and dry. Burning wet wood causes excessive buildup of creosote in the chimney and can cause fires and reduce fireplace efficiency.*

home's size, ceiling heights, floor plan, and insulation factors. Also give serious consideration to who will be operating the appliance and how it will be accomplished. The type of fuel you wish to burn is another important factor when planning for the ideal size of appliance.

*Location:* When planning for a new fireplace installation, it is wise to take a stroll through the house to get a visual idea of where the new fireplace will work the best. You'll probably find that you would prefer to locate the appliance in a heavily used area like the living room, family room or kitchen.

Usually, some structural changes will be necessary to the house itself. The changes differ from appliance to appliance. Taking a careful look of needed changes will help you decide on

*Fire appliances usually work best in the heavily used areas of your home and often become the center of family activities.*

what type of appliance is best for you and your home.

The simplest installations are

the no-vent gas fireplaces. These need only the gas line installed through the wall or floor and into the units themselves. Vented gas fireplaces can vent through any outside wall.

Wood burning fireplaces and fireplace inserts require the construction of regulation chimneys. Be sure and discuss your needs with a fire appliance professional before starting your final installation.

It is a good idea to give the availability of fuel some consideration. If you are using a wood burning unit it may be best to locate the fireplace close to the wood storage area such as a garage or closet.

Keep in mind that heat sources

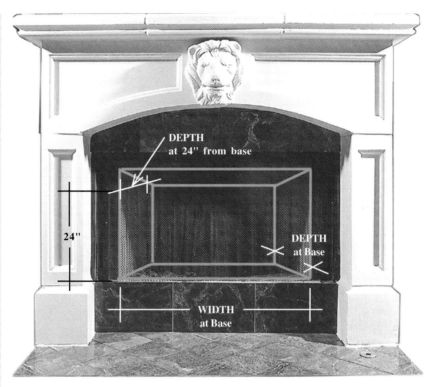

*When purchasing a new insert for an existing fireplace, you'll need the width, depth and height of the opening. Also required is the distance to the back at a 24" face height (Stone Magic).*

*With the new zero-clearance fireplace inserts just about any mantel design is totally possible. Here a stainless steel mantel surrounds a new technology insert by Superior.*

such as fireplaces work best opposite large windows that admit lots of room-warming light. This arrangement assists in evenly balancing the room's tempera-tures.

Fire appliances function most efficiently from both a social and heat efficiency standpoint when located in the main floor in the most popular gathering spots in the house. In this arrangement, units that include heat-circulating fans increase the efficiency substantially.

Be sure and locate electrical power sources such as outlets and junction boxes before your final decision.

If your home is two or more stories tall, locating the fireplace close to the stairwell will help direct warm air up the stairs to upper rooms, while pushing cool, second story air down to the first floor.

For those homes with exceptionally high ceilings, one of the new period-styled ceiling fans can assist in gently pushing accumu-lated warm air down from the ceiling into the living levels.

If your existing fireplace needs updating for efficiency you can easily install a wood or gas burning insert. Taking the inside measurements of the fireplace will be required prior to deciding what type of appliance to install.

Your measurements will need to include the height, width and depth of the fireplace opening measured at the floor of the opening. You will also need a clearance depth measurement. This measurement is obtained by making a mark on the face of the fireplace at a point 24" above the floor of the opening. At this 24" high point, measure the depth of the opening. This is necessary to calculate how high the back of the new insert must be to fit properly (see illustration above).

### *Planning for correct clearance calculations:*

Each appliance type has specific clearance requirements. Both the appliance itself and its venting system has absolute limits as to how close the heated surfaces can come to surrounding structures such as ceilings, walls and furniture. These calculations are critical for complete safety while the appliances are in operation.

It is also a good idea to contact your Homeowner's Insurance Agent before completing your planning. You may be required to update your policy and also be required to allow for an inspection by the insurance provider.

NATIONAL
FIRE ASSOCIATION
STANDARD
**211**

Almost all manufacturers refer to the National Fire Protection Association's Standard 211 (CSA or ULC in Canada) for design guidelines relating to woodburning appliances and inserts. Many of them exceed the requirements for operational

Make it of the utmost importance to follow local safety and building codes. The codes can be obtained by contacting local state, county or city government offices.

## The chimney system is a vital element in the safety and usefulness of any fire appliance.

safety and offer special designs for reducing clearance requirements using items such as double-

*Double-walled connector pipes and chimneys are available in long-lasting stainless steel. Special designs pull in combustible outside air while exhaling exhaust gases.*

walled connector pipes and mantel shielding materials.

The NFPA standards are the best in the industry, and it is wise to adhere to the details.

Keep in mind that the data concern any combustibles that are against or near the fire appliance, including clothing, newspapers and magazines, and ignition-prone fabrics used in draperies and furniture.

Remember, for the safety and sense of well-being for you and your family, nothing is more important than a safe installation of the fire appliance.

### *Chimney System, a vital element:*

To keep smoke production and creosote accumulation to a minimum, to release dangerous fumes, and to maximize heat efficiency, are the important roles of the modern chimney.

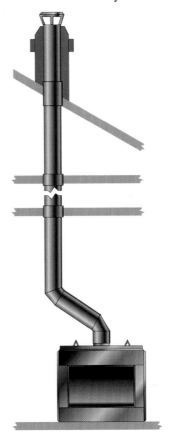

*Complete chimney installations are available in stainless steel that extend from the ports on the firebox to the outside roof. Most provide clearance panels and insulation details along with well-designed chimney caps and screens.*

*Most suppliers use mantel shielding insulation that permits the close attachment of mantel surrounds of both wood and ceramic materials.*

*Outside air creates the proper draft for efficient burning with the fuel. If poor draft is experienced, the culprit may be a too powerful ceiling fan that creates a negative draft.*

The chimney plays this vital role in the operation of any heat-producing appliance. Double-walled chimneys can do a lot more than just release the toxic exhaust gases safely away from the fire and into the outside air.

Another function is to create the draft, or air-pull that draws fresh, burnable air from outside the home into the stove to feed the fire. The air is then burned with the fuel and exhausted up the chimney. This "draft" is absolutely necessary for the efficient operation of any fire appliance. If the draft is not functioning properly, creosote is produced in damaging volumes, and an increase of environmentally dangerous smoke is released into the air.

Older chimney designs allow gases to expand and cool before they exit the chimney causing poor draft and corrosion inducing condensation. (Keep in mind that poor draft can also be caused by too low a chimney height, or from the negative pressure created by exhaust or attic fans that have been installed in heavily insulated homes.)

For your peace of mind be sure and specify EPA-Phase II approved chimneys to help insure the air safety for present and future generations. It's a smart move all around, and you'll benefit from owning a high-efficiency unit that uses a minimum amount of fuel for a maximum amount of warmth released into the occupied living areas.

For a safe and efficient chimney, consider the masterfully designed steel chimneys being offered by many suppliers. These prefabricated beauties feature corrosion-resistant flue liners, chimney connectors and chimneys. The steel is designed to endure elevated flue temperatures with lower heat requirements to allow for efficient appliance air intake. All this is accomplished with a minimum of creosote buildup. UL and UL Listed appliances are available that are rated "HT" or high temperature. These chimneys can operate at temperatures as high as 2100 degrees F. They also operate with enhanced draft, minimizing the likelihood of a blast of air coming down the chimney that can force smoke, dust and fire into the room. These chimneys can also be cleaned without moving the wood-burning appliance or insert.

Existing chimneys can be utilized when installing one of the new high-efficiency inserts. Their use will require attention. First, the chimney must be professionally inspected to ensure safe operation and compliance with the specifications of the insert.

The chimney may require a

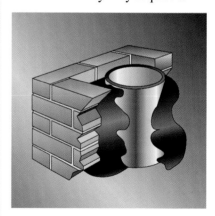

*Poured refractory relines for old chimneys are possible with new reliner forms.*

reline. A reline is literally a new liner inside the chimney itself. Relining can be accomplished by inserting a reliner form into the full length of the chimney, pouring reliner castable refractor material around the form, and removing the form. This method creates a perfect chimney liner and is a great solution for the chimney that is not up to code.

An alternative to the cast refractory reliner is the steel reliner. The steel reliner is placed inside the chimney and extends from the stove to a calculated position that is a code-specified distance from the outside surface of the roof.

*Old chimneys can experience new life with a stainless steel reliner that extends from the fireplace to the roof.*

Your local fireplace store will usually carry a complete line of steel reliners. The dealer sometimes also provides a full service for casting the refractory-type reliner, or can refer you to a local chimney professional.

Chimneys are an integral and important part of your fireplace heating system. By taking care to match your fireplace with its chimney, you ensure the peak performance of the firebox and the long-term operating safety and security of the installation.

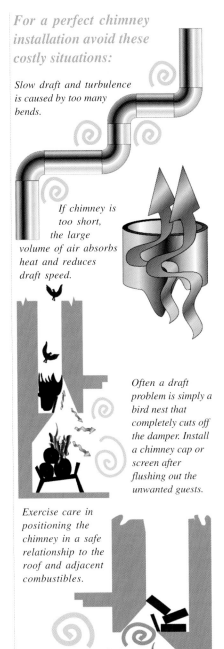

*For a perfect chimney installation avoid these costly situations:*

*Slow draft and turbulence is caused by too many bends.*

*If chimney is too short, the large volume of air absorbs heat and reduces draft speed.*

*Often a draft problem is simply a bird nest that completely cuts off the damper. Install a chimney cap or screen after flushing out the unwanted guests.*

*Exercise care in positioning the chimney in a safe relationship to the roof and adjacent combustibles.*

**Considerations for all woodburning appliances:** It is always an advantage to vent a woodburning appliance as vertically as possible. The venting can rise straight to and through the roof. Whether the venting is from the

center of the house, or up an outside wall, the chimney must extend a specified distance from the roof and surrounding constructions.

Outside installations can be the source of draft problems due to excessive cooling of the exposed chimney. This can often be corrected with a change in chimney length, or by increasing the insulation around the chimney. Other disadvantages with outside chimneys include more expensive installation and maintenance costs.

Venting from the inside of the house, and straight up through the ceiling is almost always the best design for woodburning appliances. There is an increase in performance with inside installations, and also a decrease in construction costs.

Several types of stainless steel chimneys are available for ceiling and outside wall installations. Double-wall pipe is available that allows you to construct the chimney closer to combustible materials than the single wall chimneys.

The floors immediately surrounding the firebox also need fireproof protection. The needs

*This Heat-N-Glo insert is enhanced by a large off-floor fireproof hearth-pad. Ceramic tile surfaces are also ideal for floor protection.*

for this type of precaution vary from appliance to appliance. Open faced wood-burning units require a large hearth-pad to catch sparks and cinders that pop from the fire. Even glass-doored units require the same consideration when the doors are opened while adjusting the burning fire.

Your local fireplace dealer can assist you in planning the proper hearth-pad size. For a stylish and classic hearth-pad, consider using ceramic, marble or stone tile. An endless variety of colors and textures are available that will go with any period mantel, and will satisfy any taste.

Chimneys must extend at least 3 feet above the roof where it breaks through the roof, and must

*Exercise great care in positioning the chimney top, to the roof and surrounding combustibles.*

be built at a distance of at least 10 feet from any other construction adjacent to it on any side. Keep in mind that the dimensions listed are minimum dimensions. Your particular chimney may require a greater length for proper draft and appliance operation.

***Chimney maintenance:*** The National Fire Protection Association suggests that all chimney types be inspected and cleaned once per year. Any buildup of creosote over 1/4" thick must be removed by cleaning thoroughly. Creosote builds up over time and can become a real fire hazard. A heavy buildup can ignite, turning the chimney into a giant blow torch that will destroy the chimney and often the house it is attached to. Firewood with a high moisture content can increase creosote buildup, so be sure and check inside your chimney for a few days after burning this type of wood.

In conclusion, it is best to call a professional chimney sweep to service your chimneys. They are fast and efficient, and possess the machinery and tools to do a thorough and safe cleaning.

Gas-fired appliances do not create a creosote buildup in the chimney. However, a regularly scheduled checkup annually of the burners, controls, venting systems and electrical connections is necessary to maintain peak performance, efficiency and safety.

*In conclusion, with all wood burning appliances it is extremely important to keep creosote buildup to a minimum. To accomplish this, a robust, fully burning, self-sustained start-up fire is the best and safest approach.*

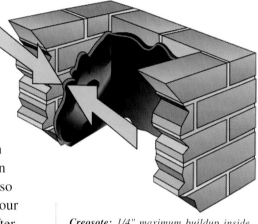

*Creosote: 1/4" maximum buildup inside chimney allocated by the EPA. Keeping chimneys free of creosote prevents fires.*

*Burning wood with a moisture content of below 25%, and burning hotter, smaller fires will substantially reduce the creosote buildup in your chimney. If fire dies, restart using kindling to maintain proper chimney temperatures and draft.*

*In addition, ash removal is a critical maintenance requirement of all wood-burning appliances. You can stir old ashes among the hot ashes to burn them more thoroughly, thus reducing the volume of ash to be disposed of. Always store ash in a metal container with a secure lid, on fireproof surfaces, and away from flammable materials. Remember, cooled ash is dense in lime and potash, and makes a great garden fertilizer for healthy compost piles.*

# Common Fireplace Terms

Understanding these terms will insure that you and the professionals understand each other, and will also increase the quality, efficiency and economy of your installation. It will also help increase your confidence as you begin planning for your fireplace installation.

When discussing your firebox needs with the professionals, one of the most used of the acronyms is the AFUE, or the Annual Fuel Utilization Efficiency developed by the U.S. Department of Energy. The higher the AFUE rating, the more efficient the appliance. The rating reflects the heat output compared to the fuel input.

Most appliances will have a published BTU Output, which is a good measuring device when calculating the amount of heat required to warm a specific area. (A BTU is the amount of energy required to heat one pint of water 1 degree Fahrenheit.)

BTU Input is an important consideration for a gas appliance, and indicates the amount of fuel consumed in one hour. To calculate the appliance's efficiency, you simply divide the BTU Output by the BTU Input.

Burn Time represents the amount of wood fuel burned by an appliance with one fuel load. For example, you'll need this info when fueling up for long-term fires that are expected to burn throughout the night.

Catalytic Combustor is a wood-fireplace appliance accessory that helps your fuel burn cleanly and efficiently. They are a replacement item and last approximately 10,000 burning hours.

The Chimney is the passage through which smoke and gases escape from a fireplace and is sometimes referred to as the flue. It is usually vertical, and rises above the roof by a critical distance.

Creosote Buildup takes place inside the chimney and consists of deposits from the fire smoke. Burning wood that is not dry contributes to this phenomenon.

The cubic volume of a woodburning appliance is measured in Firebox Capacity, and is needed when calculating how much wood can be inserted for a full load.

The Fireplace or Firebox is an open recess for holding a fire at the base of a chimney and is sometimes incorrectly referred to as the hearth.

Fireplace Inserts are manufactured fireboxes that are inserted into existing fireplaces to increase efficiency and safety. Gas and woodburning types are available.

The Hearth is the floor of a fireplace, usually extending into the room and is paved with brick, flagstone or cement. It is sometimes raised above the room floor.

Heating Capacity is calculated to reflect the number of square feet or cubic feet of actual living space that can be heated by the appliance.

The Overall Efficiency of a woodburning appliance is calculated by averaging the combustion and heat transfer efficiencies. The highest published efficiencies reflect the most economical to operate woodburning appliances.

The Oregon Department of Environmental Quality has created charts that are easy to use and that will save you a lot of figuring. Note: The type and condition of the wood you are burning will effect efficiency.

The economic efficiency of operating a gas appliance is expressed as the Steady State Efficiency, which reflects how economically the fuel is transferred into heat.

The Vented Fireplace Insert requires a chimney or exhaust for smoke and fumes. Top vented, side vented and rear vented styles are available.

A No Vent Fireplace is designed for the safe use of all combustible materials with no fumes. These devices require no chimney, flue or exhaust ports and can be placed in almost any environment.

# Step-by-Step Fireplace Installation for Placement in Existing Rooms

Some advance planning can make most any do-it-yourself fireplace installation easy and fun. Pre-planning, combined with a few dozen spare-time hours will provide you, your family and friends the comfort and warmth of a real fire.

Sharing your planning with your local fireplace dealer will ensure a safe installation that will meet all local building codes and requirements.

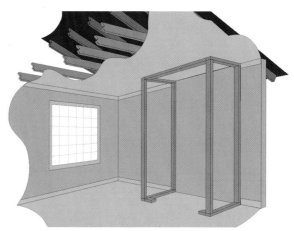

3. Using standard 2" x 4" studs, frame in the outside area of the installation. The two short blocks on the floor actually bump up against the steel firebox. The width between them equals the width of the firebox.

1. Planning begins by targeting a desired location for the fireplace. Locating the installation close to a large window will help offset the heat loss from large areas of exposed glass. Next, obtain proper building permits.

4. Set the insert without the chimney in place ensuring that all suggested clearances are allowed for. Install the optional outside combustible air kit. Secure the firebox solidly to the frame and floor.

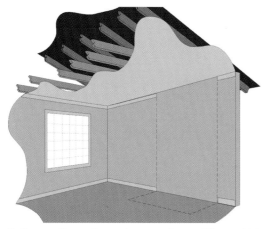

2. Prepare the work area by removing molding and trim based on the fireplace installation dimensions. Next, use masking tape to mark off the exact area of the installation on the floor, ceiling and walls.

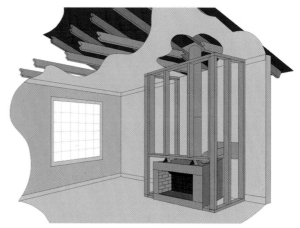

5. Make saw cuts to ceiling and roof members carefully following the manufacturer's guidelines and local building codes provided when obtaining the building permits. Complete the framework and install the chimney.

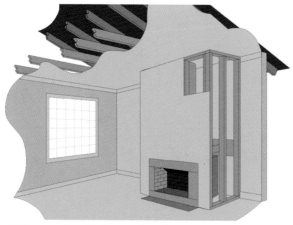

6. Many modern fireboxes allow for zero-clearance installation of surrounding building materials. Continue by applying drywall or paneling to the framework as shown. Finish drywall by taping, spackling and sanding.

7. Following the completion of the wall surface installation, the matching molding and trim is added to the new fireplace area. This installation features a ceramic tile surround applied around the opening.

8. This do-it-yourself mantel is designed for easy construction and can be cut from standard high density particle board, pine or hardwood. All cuts can be made on a standard table or radial arm saw.

9. The simplicity of this design is timeless, and is appropriate for a variety of installations. The unit is assembled and finishes applied prior to attaching it to the wall surrounding the firebox.

10. Next, the mantel is attached securely to the wall and framework that immediately surrounds the firebox. There are a large variety of fireplace mantels and surrounds that can be incorporated with this scheme.

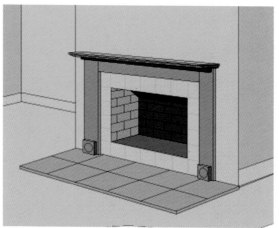

11. The finished custom installation features a steel firebox with actual refractory brick in the fire chamber giving an authentic aura to a dramatic installation. Mantels can be chosen from a wide variety of designs.

*Superior Fireplace Company*

# Chapter Three

# Wood-Fired Fireplaces

## Traditional and High-Efficiency Woodburning Fireplaces

## The latest firebox designs are better than ever and provide a variety of attractive options. Many surpass even the EPA's high quality standards.

For the purist, the masonry or steel traditional woodburning fireplace is economical to install and provides a beautiful and natural fire.

The Environmental Protection Agency has had a tremendously positive impact on the quality and efficiency of heating appliances. Uncertified appliances have about a 50% overall efficiency, while EPA-certified appliances all have a 70% or higher rating, while at the same time reduce pollution by 85%, and with woodburners, reduce refueling costs up to 30%. Another real plus is the increased cleanliness and ease of maintenance of the new designs.

The EPA applied the restrictions to woodburning appliances to help preserve the environment. In one five-year period, the certified appliances burned 700,000 less cords of wood than would have been burned with regular units, saving a forest consisting of thousands of acres.

700,000 cords of wood saved in five year period.

This reduced the amount of pollutants released into the air by over 400,000 tons!

When shopping for a new appliance, keep in mind that the retailer can only display and sell catalytic appliances that release a maximum of 4.1 grams per hour, and noncatalytic units that release a maximum of 7.5 grams per hour. In some cases, certain appliances are not required to have an EPA certification. These include some furnaces, masonry stoves, masonry fireplaces, coal-fired and gas-fired units.

*EPA restrictions reduced pollution by 400,000 tons in just five years.*

*Uncertified appliances that have a 50% overall efficiency emit high levels of pollutions into the air.*

*EPA certified appliances have 70% or greater rating and reduce pollution by 85%.*

The traditional masonry or steel fireplace is perfect for glamour looks where beauty is the focus and the aesthetic ambiance dominates the mood of the presentation.

*Superior's ESTATE is the largest factory-built fireplace ever offered. This unit is for installations of a grand scale. Its firebox is so huge that it can best be measured in feet rather than inches: 4 feet across the front, 3 feet wide across the rear, 2 feet deep, with over 7 square feet of interior hearth area. It is perfect for country manors, stately residences and luxury homes.*

***Factory-built traditional woodburners.*** In new installations, the standard manufactured steel woodburning fireplace and chimneys are a first choice for many homeowners who are installing a firebox for the first time. Fireplace doors are optional but not necessarily a part of the installation. This traditional approach to providing a living fire is the most economical to install, is safe and reliable, and does not require an EPA rating. Efficiency averages are much lower than the EPA-certified fireplace inserts. Manufacturers' installation requirements vary greatly from supplier to supplier. Check the installation literature provided with the manufactured fireplace to plan safety-oriented framing and

*Traditionals are 10% to 30% efficient.*

facing installations.

**Caution:** Some manufacturers require additional metal strips to be installed in front of and under certain units. Be sure and check out the details with a professional.

Superior Fireplace Company of Fullerton, California, offers a manufactured fireplace that is truly on a grand scale. The firebox is a huge 4 feet wide by 2 feet deep by over 2 feet tall. The design features realistic traditional masonry. The massive iron grate can hold a half dozen very large logs all at the same time. Superior also manufactures standard-sized fireplaces incorporating the high quality tradition. Efficient outside air kits are offered, as well as

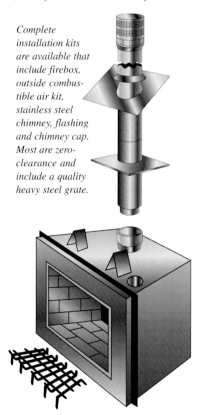

*Complete installation kits are available that include firebox, outside combustible air kit, stainless steel chimney, flashing and chimney cap. Most are zero-clearance and include a quality heavy steel grate.*

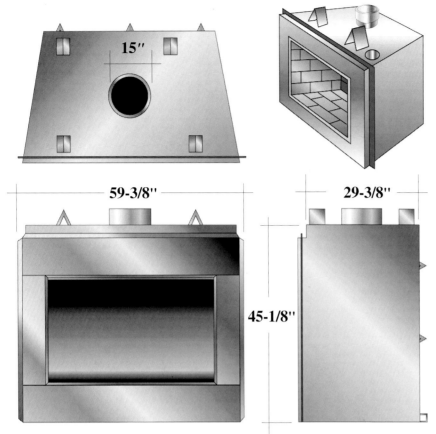

*Superior glass doors are offered in a variety of high quality styles.*

*Superior's Estate manufactured fireplace features an incredibly realistic traditional masonry refractory. Recessed screen pockets and a clean face design produce a 48" x 28" rock to screen opening. An integral, masonry look, inclined ash lip is flush with the front opening. The Estate's massive iron grate is capable of holding a half dozen very large logs at once.*

finely trimmed glass doors. This is one of the best manufactured alternatives to a large, custom-built masonry fireplace, and the beautiful masonry look of the firebox design works perfectly with stone, cast masonry or wood mantels.

Remember, when installing a traditional fireplace, glass doors can help keep heat in the house by preventing the warm room air from exiting through the damper.

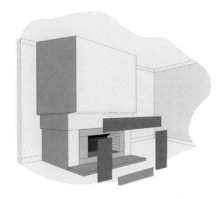

*The Superior Fireplace Company installation shown at right can be reproduced by boxing in the fireplace as shown above. Once drywall is applied, sanded and finished, a high pressure laminate like Formica is applied in a stone or metal surface. The end result is a dramatically modern and easily maintained mantel. The new technology steel fireplaces allow this type of construction due to the zero-clearance features of the best designs. An alternative to the high pressure laminate would be a fine hardwood veneer with a semigloss polyurethane catalyst finish.*

*Superior Fireplace Company*

The all-steel high efficiency wood burning fireplace or insert is a perfect combination of high technology, clean aesthetics, comfort and convenience.

They are always manufactured with heat-saving glass doors and electrically powered heat circulating fans. These latest inserts are easily installed into most masonry and zero clearance fireplaces, and provide a beautiful, heat-producing fire with a minimum of effort and a maximum of creature comfort and convenience. New stainless steel fire

chimneys can be installed. As an option, existing masonry chimneys can be relined with steel refiners, or with the poured refractory refiners that can be built to match exactly with your new insert's flue diameter. In this field, Heat-N-Glo and Superior are paving the way in innovation, quality and customer service.

The Heat-N-Glo line of woodburning inserts includes a clean burning system that is unique in today's market and has passed all four phases of the EPA Phase II testing. The EPA approval allows it to be installed in areas where wood-burning restrictions apply.

The wood burning high-efficiency units are always manufactured with heat-preserving glass doors, and electrically powered heat blowers. There are several quality producers of high efficiency fireplaces including:

**Lennox**
**Regency**
**Heat-N-Glo**
**Lopi**
**Superior**
**Austroflamm**
**Fireplace**
**Xtrordinair**
**Mendota**
**Kozy Heat**

The addresses of the listed suppliers are in the appendix in the back of the book.

Most of the fireplaces allow extremely creative installations. Various

*Heat-N-Glo inserts work well in this quietly traditional setting that incorporates a custom off-the-shelf mantel.*

venting strategies allow fireplace installations on an interior or exterior wall. Top-vent and direct-vent fireplaces are designed for installations in areas like the basement that cannot use a back-venting direct vent.

In addition, the appliances

*Heat-N-Glo inserts are available with a large variety of stylish surrounds. This model is a simulated marble look that is appropriate in almost any setting.*

maintain indoor air quality and are not affected by house depressurization. The direct-vent designs have a sealed combustion chamber, using 100 percent outside air for combustion and exhausting 100 percent of all combustion products. This means that there is

*Heat-N-Glo provided the high-efficiency insert for this grandly dramatic presentation. High-efficiency units provide adequate heat for large areas, and often are as efficient as a forced-air gas furnace.*

no exchange of combustion air and room air and that no combustion by-product pollutants are allowed into the home. These fireplace inserts do not contribute to negative pressure problems so common in today's tightly sealed homes.

With fuel-burning efficiencies of 80 percent and greater, the inserts are clean-burning, use a minimum amount of fuel, and are cost-effective. Many even operate during electrical power failures. And if you are in a clean-burn area, many high-efficiency fireplaces will meet all regulations.

When planning the installation of a high-efficiency woodburning fire appliance, be sure and work with your local fireplace dealer to obtain all the necessary specifications and local governmental installation regulations.

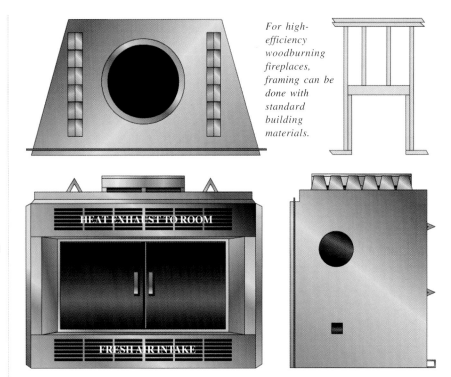

*For high-efficiency woodburning fireplaces, framing can be done with standard building materials.*

HEAT EXHAUST TO ROOM

FRESH AIR INTAKE

*Several suppliers provide quality high-efficiency wood fireplaces and inserts. All are manufactured of high-grade steels and include tight-fitting glass doors. Features include intake and exhaust fans for efficient circulation of air. Venting can be on the left or right side, off the top or out the back of the units. The best woodburning units include stainless steel chimney kits and have absolutely realistic ceramic logs that feature permanent natural-looking hot glowing ashes.*

*High-efficiency wood-burner chimneys can exhaust from the top, rear or sides.*

*Some manufacturers offer high-efficiency units that are over 80% efficient.*

*High-efficiency units can protrude to the outside or be built into an inside box-in that requires no new foundationing.*

*Gas and wood inserts allow zero-clearance application of mantels and surrounds. This simple installation includes a readily available ceramic tile surround with a custom-made mantel. The mantel is of lumber yard materials and mouldings and is easily built and installed.*

*The Rumford fireplace is ideal for traditional installations. Note the stately proportions of the refractory brick-lined firebox.*

The Rumford brick and mortar fireplace was designed over 200 years ago and is still the only masonry design that meets the EPA's environment-saving pollution standards.

***Masonry Fireplaces:*** Of all the classic masonry designs we've reviewed over the past few years, the Rumford fireplace stands out as the most efficient and well-designed. Superior Clay Corp. of Uhrichsville, Ohio, and inventor and professor Jim Buckley have teamed up to produce the astounding masonry Buckley-Rumford fireplace kits based on the 1796 A.D. designs of the eccentric inventor, Count Rumford.

*"With the assistance of the following plain and simple instructions, the chimneys will never fail to answer, venture I say even beyond expectation. The room will be heated more pleasantly with less than half the fuel used before...", Rumford wrote in 1796.*

Purists love the Rumford fireplace. It was designed over two centuries ago and is still the only mortar and brick design that completely meets the EPA's pollution standards.

*The following article, "Reviving the Rumford," by Jim Buckley was printed in the Journal of Light Construction.*

A true Rumford fireplace is recognizable by its shallow firebox, angled side walls, and perfectly straight back. No fireplace heats better than a Rumford. Now, manufactured components make this classic design easier to build.

Count Rumford's elegant fireplace became the state of the art within months of its invention in the late 1700s. Unfortunately, even though thousands of Rumford fireplaces were built, few people understood the principles behind Rumford's

design. When wood heat went out of vogue around 1850, Rumford's ideas were diluted by the furious competition to design and patent popular coalburning fireplaces. And shortly after gas fireplaces replaced coal in the 1890s, wood fireplaces virtually disappeared from American homes.

Wood-burning fireplaces became popular again in the 1920s – almost 170 years after the last Rumfords were built, and by 1950 the modern fireplace had been reinvented as a result of the standardization of modern building codes. But by that time, a number of mistaken notions about the Rumford had become so popular that most of the fireplaces, including Rumfords, that are built

**Rumford-Buckley Fireplace**
**Figure 1.** *The Rumford-Buckley design has a shallow back and steeply angled sides that radiate heat outward into the room.*

**Traditional Fireplace**
*The deep back and shallow-angle sides of the traditional fireplace radiate turbulent air and less heat into the room.*

in America were modified in ways that were less than improvements on Rumford's design.

Most modern fireplaces are built as a nostalgic luxury, producing lots of smoke and not much heat (see Figure 1, page 29). But the Rumford fireplace is making a comeback. Its clean, simple lines are attracting more buyers and its effective use of radiant heat makes it a real fireplace to warm yourself by.

And while other fireplaces draw lots of warm interior air up the chimney, the aerodynamic Rumford burns cleaner and wastes less heat.

### The Secret of the Rumford.

Science has come a long way since Rumford's day. Our modern understanding of heat and air flow is being applied to build Rumford fireplaces the way he designed them – with straight backs and rounded throats.

Compared with a conventional modern fireplace, the Rumford draws better, burns cleaner, and radiates more heat. The Rumford's curved throat and straight back create a steady draft in which combustion gases and room air stay separate and flow smoothly through the small damper. That's why the unique design works so well.

By contrast, the sloped back of a conventional fireplace creates a turbulent mix of room air and combustion gases. This design, in contrast to Rumford's ingenious design, cools the gases and creates drag, slowing the draft and requiring a larger damper opening.

*Radiant heat.* Rumford realized that the only useful heat a fireplace produces is radiant heat (in fact, Rumford coined the phrase "radiant heat"). The heated air from a fire goes up the chimney, but the radiant heat projects out into the room. Rumford thought the firewalls of a fireplace reflected the heat out; that's why he recommended whitewashing the inside of the fireplace. We now know that the fireplace walls, whether white or black, absorb the heat and then reradiate it. But either way, the angled walls in a shallow Rumford direct radiant heat out

into the room much better than a deep, square fireplace does.

*Streamlining.* But shallow fireplaces tend to smoke, especially when they're wide and tall like the Rumford. To solve that problem, Rumford measured and recorded temperatures of only 75°F near the rounded throat; just 2 inches away near the back, we recorded 730°F! As we suspected, the room air coming in over the fire in a Rumford doesn't mix with the hot products of combustion. Instead, the room air acts as an invisible glass door that keeps the smoke behind it as they both go up the throat together.

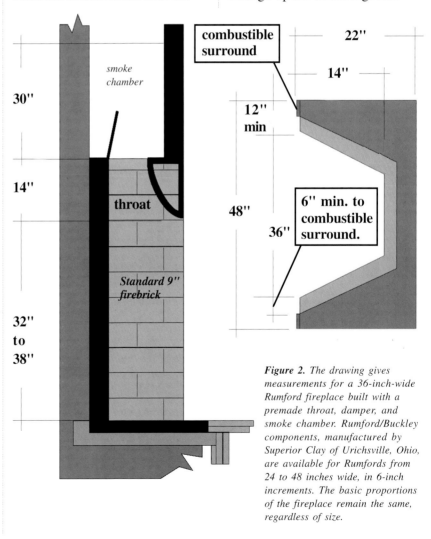

**Figure 2.** *The drawing gives measurements for a 36-inch-wide Rumford fireplace built with a premade throat, damper, and smoke chamber. Rumford/Buckley components, manufactured by Superior Clay of Urichsville, Ohio, are available for Rumfords from 24 to 48 inches wide, in 6-inch increments. The basic proportions of the fireplace remain the same, regardless of size.*

This laminar type of air flow – where gases move in smooth streams without mixing turbulently – reduces drag. That's why aircraft and automobile designers strive to create laminar flow. In the throat of a fireplace, laminar flow allows the smoke to escape easily into the chimney.

***The Rumford is a real surprise for almost every builder.*** Most masons who build modern fireplaces won't believe a Rumford will draw until they see it happen with their own eyes. The rules are different for the two types of fireplaces.

In a modern fireplace, the fireback is usually sloped toward the front, casting the products of combustion forward. Incoming room air spills over the edge of a lintel and mixes turbulently with the smoke. Most masons will tell you that you need to drop the lintel 8 or 9 inches below the damper to create a pocket for this smoke and incoming room air to "roll." Otherwise, the fireplace will smoke.

But all this turbulence is inefficient. The rolling smoke and air need a huge throat to get through. A Rumford fireplace operates on a different principle. The straight back lets smoke from the fire travel straight up into the chimney. The curved throat, unlike a square lintel, lets room air pass smoothly and swiftly over the fire and into the flue. The result is that the modern Rumford with an opening a foot taller needs a throat that is less than half the size of a regular

fireplace's.

***Building the Rumford.*** The key to building a well functioning Rumford fireplace is to stick to Count Rumford's original design. His instructions explain how to carefully lay out the shallow firebox with a plumb bob using the special jigs he developed. Rumford recommended plaster to achieve smooth, rounded curves at the throat.

Nowadays, you can get modern manufactured components that save a lot of time. The method Jim Buckley helped develop uses a manufactured

throat and smoke chamber. Each of his components is carefully engineered and crafted for generations of efficient, safe and beautiful fires. The components are produced commercially by Superior Clay Corporation.

*Figure 3. The throat sits in refractory mortar at the top of a Rumford firebox.*

***The firebox.*** Build the Rumford firebox using standard 9-inch firebrick and refractory mortar. Although a Rumford can be built to almost any size, the proportions stay roughly the same. Figure 2 (page 30), shows a 36-inch-wide fireplace. Rumford fireplaces are usually about as tall as they are wide, but you can adjust the height by a few inches. A slightly shorter opening makes the fireplace draw better, especially when

*Figure 4. The cast iron damper mounts directly on top of the curved throat component of a Rumford firebox.*

a small fire is built in a large fireplace.

The side walls of the firebox are angled inward no more than 135 degrees off the back wall. Use refractory mortar to lay the firebrick. The firebox walls should be at least 8 inches thick, so back up the firebrick with solid masonry. Pack any voids full of ordinary mortar.

**Throat and damper.** Set the curved Rumford throat in refractory mortar on top of the firebox (Figure 3, page 31). Lay up surrounding masonry to the top of the throat, packing the throat solid with ordinary mortar as you go.

The throat is designed to carry the load, but place a length of rebar in the first thick mortar joint above the front edge of the throat to provide an extra margin of safety. Set the cast iron damper in a bed of mortar over the throat opening (Figure 4, page 31). Make sure the valve plate can open and close freely. Close the valve.

**Smoke chamber.** You have some leeway in positioning the smoke chamber (Figure 5, above) over the damper. Line it up with where you want the flue to be, but check again to be sure that the damper valve can still open and close freely.

After surrounding the smoke chamber with masonry at least 4 inches thick, you are ready to set the first flue tile. Build the rest of the chimney just as you would any other chimney.

**The Surround.** As with any fireplace, Rumford surrounds should be at least 6 inches wide, which keep combustible materials

*Figure 5. The Rumford firebox and smoke chamber is now ready for the chimney construction.*

away from the source of heat and flame. Rumford surrounds should be almost flush with the wall of the room. Any masonry that projects around the side of the fireplace will block some of the radiant heat. At the top of the fireplace opening, bring the surround material just low enough to cover the edge of the throat, but maintain the streamlined curve of the throat.

This curve is like the leading edge of an airplane wing. You will ruin the air flow if you drop a header several inches below the opening. Again, try to avoid a brick surround that requires an angled

lintel to support the header, because that would make it hard to maintain the streamlining.

**Glass doors.** Rumford fireplaces don't need glass doors, but if you choose to have them, mount the doors on the outside surface of the surround so that the lines of the covings and the curved throat are not interrupted. Since glass blocks about 80 percent of radiant heat, open the doors when the fire is lit. The scientific data is not yet available to put numbers on the Rumford's comparative efficiency; but anyone who owns a well-made Rumford can tell you that lighting a fire in a Rumford is a great way to warm up a room. If you haven't tried it, you don't know what you're missing.

*Jim Buckley, of Seattle, Washington, has been a mason for 15 years and has built more than 600 Rumford fireplaces.*

*Count Rumford was born Benjamin Thompson in Woburn, Mass., in 1753. He picked the wrong side in the American Revolution and had to leave suddenly with the British. For his work on the subject of fireplaces, the Bavarian government gave him the title of Count of the Holy Roman Empire.*

*Thomas Jefferson read Rumford's essays within months after they were published and switched to building Rumford fireplaces at Monticello. By 1834, Henry Thoreau's Walden listed a Rumford fireplace as one of the comforts taken for granted by modern man.*

*But wrong ideas about Rumford fireplaces were introduced right from the beginning by others, and have been passed along up to the present day. For example, the mistaken notion that the purpose of the "smoke shelf" is to block downdrafts in the back of the chimney was first put forward in 1796 by Thomas Danforth in an essay "fully explaining" Rumford.*

*His essays are out of print now, but you can still find them in libraries: Look for the Collected Works of Count Rumford, Vol: II, edited by Sanborn Brown. – J.B.*

Step by Step details for constructing the efficient and modern Rumford/Buckley woodburning brick fireplace:

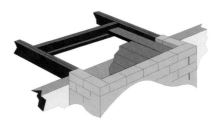

*1. Hearth base and foundation.* A solid masonry hearth base 4" thick should be supported on an adequate masonry foundation. The base must be deep enough front to back to support the fireplace and chimney. The face is typically flush with the inside wall.

*2. Framing around the fireplace.* Combustibles are to be kept at least 2" away from the outside of a masonry fireplace or chimney. The opening in the combustible wall is 4" wider than the masonry, with the header 3' above the top of the fireplace opening.

*3. Inner hearth.* Lay the firebrick on masonry hearth base using refractory mortar. Make joints minimum 1/16" between firebrick. The firebrick inner hearth is just big enough so the firebrick box can be laid on top of this firebrick inner hearth.

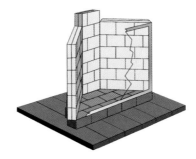

*4. Building the firebox.* Set, level and brace the steel frame of the glass door (provided with Superior Clay kit) on the hearth where the rough firebrick opening is positioned at a point flush with the inside house wall. Build the firebox using standard 9" refractory brick.

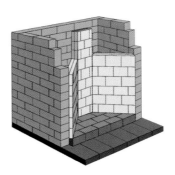

*5. Constructing the backup block.* The firebrick is backed up with solid masonry creating a firebox wall at least 8" thick. The bricks or concrete blocks are woven together at the corners for strength. Fill the space between the block and the firebrick with ordinary mortar.

*6. Setting the throat.* Thread the throat tiles onto a steel angle iron provided in the kit

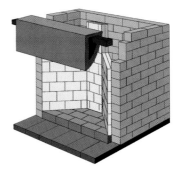

and set the throat as a unit on the block bearing surfaces. Align the bottom edge of the throat against the door frame template. Work refractory mortar into the joints. Remember, the masonry throat opening dimensions are critical.

A full set of installation instructions is available from Superior Clay Corporation.

Many accessories, both decorative and functional, exist to make your hearth more usable and beautiful.

*Fireplace Accessories.* The timeless beauty of the hearth is enhanced by accessories that reflect the taste and life-style of the homeowner. Accessories also add an element of interest and surprise even when the fire is extinguished. There is a wide array of accessories available in today's market to suit every need and taste. Traditional items are plentiful and well designed, as are the contemporary and modern accessories. There are so many ways to accessorize to express your personality that you'll no doubt spend many enjoyable hours adding little treasures to the collection of keepsakes around the fire.

*Protective Firescreens.* Firescreens come in a selection of materials, styles and sizes to fit any fireplace opening. You can select from delicately designed metal screens and highly artistic etched and beveled glass masterpieces.

What's more, a stylish firescreen will add an elegant touch to your presentation during and after the fire. You can choose from one to four paneled screens that will protect the surrounding floors, constructions and furnishings from being affected by flying embers and sparks.

*Fireplace Glass Doors.* Prevention of heat loss is the major goal of any glass door addition. Doorless fireplaces allow the chimney, when the damper is open, to draw warmed room air immediately up the flue to the outside. Of course, the fire has to be completely extinguished before the damper is closed. Waiting for the embers to die out has caused many a homeowner to forget to close the damper at the end of the fireburning session. The open damper will literally allow all the room heat to be drawn up the chimney.

The glass doors prevent this after-fire heat loss. You simply close the doors when leaving the

fireside. This prevents room heat from being lost up the chimney. It is wise to leave the doors closed whenever there is no fire in the firebox. Most dampers warp with time and do not close tightly. The loose fit allows a continual heat loss up the flue. Because of this, many states now require that all new fireplaces are fitted with glass doors.

Finally, one of the really useful features of every glass door installation is the protection from sparks, soot, dust and flying embers. Many designs help you control the flames with draft controls that limit incoming air.

*Fireplace Grates.* A wide variety of grate types are available.

Designers have developed highly efficient self-fueling multilevel grates that add convenience while increasing efficiency through increased air circulation under the logs. You can also purchase standard grates of cast iron or

welded steel. Grates keep the wood up off the refractory floor, allowing for increased air circulation and burning consistency.

***Fireplace Gloves.*** This is a real necessity for the wood burning enthusiast. A good set of gloves with a long gauntlet  prevents burns, and keeps the hands soft and free from scratches and splinters from handling firewood.

***Firesets.*** The woodburning hearthside benefits greatly from the presence of a well designed

fireset. Firesets assist in making wood adjustments and cleanup a pleasure. Many styles are available in cast iron, pewter and

plated or solid brass. Also available are bases and fenders in striking designs. Even though firesets are designed for wood burning installations, some will find the addition of a fireset to a gas-fired fireplace a pleasing and realistic addition.

***Firestarters.*** Matches, lighters, firestarters of fatwood are all necessary luxuries for the woodburning fireplace enthusiast. For barbecues and campfires, you can start a fire in seconds using fatwood, a high-resin natural kindling. Combined with long matches or long-handled gas lighters, you'll be equipped to start ignition on demand.

***Hearth Rugs.*** It is easy to protect your floors and carpets from sparks and embers with a fireproof hearth rug. The new styles are fireproof and come in a stylish variety of colors and textures.

***Wood Carriers.*** Wood handles of dowels or canvas wraps make wood carriers ideal for helping you bring in wood for the fire.

Little wood carts on antique-styled wheels are also available. Fireside wood rings are also a smart investment, providing ample storage in a variety of styles and sizes.

***Steamers and Trivets.*** Cast iron trivets are great for warming drinks and treats by the fire. Steamers help add moisture to the air during burning making the room seem warmer.

***Bellows.*** For wood burning installations, these are especially useful when starting a new fire, or reviving a dying one. The increase of oxygen provided will instantly grow new flames.

***Firebacks.*** Cast iron firebacks are available for wood burning fireplaces in both Early American and contem-

porary designs. Firebacks help protect the refractory materials in the firebox while at the same time increasing radiant heat.

*Superior Fireplace Company High-Efficiency Gas Insert and installation.*

# Chapter Four

# Gas-Fired Fireplaces

## High-Efficiency units for existing and new installations.

**Modern gas fireplaces are extremely clean and economical to install and operate. Many provide the ultimate in convenience using programmable remote controls. All are environmentally safe and deliver heat at extremely high efficiencies.**

The authentic look and warmth of a wood fire is the standard for today's new gas fireplaces and inserts. And, with the addition of remote control, you'll enjoy the ultimate in comfort and convenience. Remember those cold mornings when you just did not want to get out of bed? A gas fireplace in the bedroom is easily possible, and you'll be able to start the fire without leaving the comfort of your covers.

The new gas fireplaces, logs and inserts are so realistic that you cannot tell whether they are wood or gas. Efficiencies are 70% and higher and equal today's best forced air gas furnaces using

*Gas appliance efficiency is 70% and higher.*

America's most popular and least expensive fuel, natural gas.

The great advantage to a natural gas appliance is the option of placing the appliance virtually anywhere in the home with a minimum of space requirements. Gas appliances are designed zero-clearance, allowing you to place the unit in the chosen area and build up adjoining walls around it. The newest designs allow for vertical, back or side venting. There are even freestanding vent-free gas-fired fireplaces that consume all exhaust fumes and can fit virtually anywhere in any room.

The conventional chimney is no longer required with the new

*Gas inserts can bring new life to an old fireplace. For existing chimneys, kits meet the most stringent EPA standards and come complete with new stainless steel chimney liners. Gas fireplaces are often more efficient than gas furnaces.*

gas technology. A real plus of the venting systems of today's gas models is the direct-vent feature. This ingenious design allows the outside combustion air to be

The new gas appliances are dramatic additions to any room. The dramatic improvements rival the heat efficiency and safety of the best forced-air gas furnaces.

*Sealed glass fronts and long-lasting stainless steel chimneys are typical with high efficiency gas appliances.*

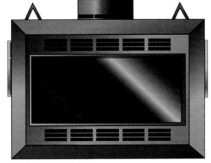

*Gas inserts fit comfortably into existing fireplace fireboxes and are a great way to add glamour to a room while increasing the heat efficiency of the fireplace.*

drawn into the heat chamber, and the exhaust fumes to be exited directly and horizontally through exterior walls.

If you desire a real brick look for the fire chamber to add to the installation's authenticity, fireboxes are available that are built using real refractory brick. The

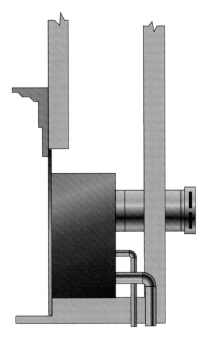

*If you are adding a room or building a new home, gas appliances work well with new fireplace installations. Standard framing methods are employed with zero-clearance possible on most models.*

authenticity can be enhanced with the addition of one of a wide variety of mantel choices that include wood, tile, stone and brick designs.

The designers have done their homework on today's classic styles. Finishes are of an extremely high grade and can be obtained in a wide variety of materials, textures and colors from enamel to antique brass. The logs themselves are so well designed only the expert can tell them from the real thing. You can choose from a large selection on wood species including oak, birch, and driftwood in many different configurations. The best designs include permanent burning embers and glowing ashes that completely mimic those of an actual fire, and that are never consumed.

The most astounding feature of the new gas fires are the flames

that equal burning wood in color and beauty. The new yellow flame designs have been tested and approved by the American and Canadian Gas Associations, and

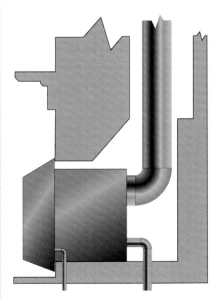

*Today's high-efficiency gas appliances can be placed in almost any setting. Top, side, and rear venting is available. Units feature warm air circulation fans for increased efficiency and draw combustible air into the firebox from the outside. All have sealed glass fronts and clean-burn features.*

also by the U.S. Underwriters Laboratories, and are completely safe. The latest designs use flame rods or refining fuel to create the wood fire look and have the added feature of varying color and movement that exactly duplicate a wood fire.

When installing any gas appliance you must have the assistance of a certified professional. Contact your local fireplace dealer for more information, or refer to the list of dealers in the appendix for a professional near you.

*Gas logs are an easy and economical alternative for creating a maintenance-free gas fireplace from an existing wood fireplace installation.*

Gas Logs are an ideal method for upgrading an existing wood fireplace. They're a great buy and are easy to install.

You can easily upgrade your old wood fireplace with a real wood fire look with one of the new, highly authentic Gas Log appliances. The units are considered decorative only, yet provide the authentic glow and aura

desired from a roaring fire. Installations are easy on you and your budget. Operation is simple, and lighting can be accomplished with a match or with a push-button control. And even though gas logs are certified as decorative, they will equal or exceed the efficiency of a woodburning open fireplace.

A great advantage of a gas log installation is the low maintenance required. There is no creosote buildup to contend with, and no bark, ash or wood chips to dispose of. It's a great way to enjoy the comfort of a living fire without the necessity of hauling and chopping wood. If natural gas is not available in your area, many manufacturers offer models

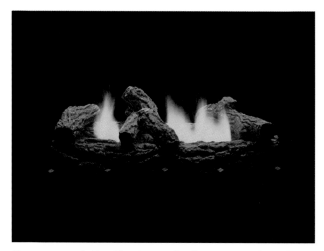

*You can economically add to the appeal and convenience of a tired old wood fireplace with one of the classic new gas log sets like this beauty from Heat-N-Glo. The gas logs are as efficient as the old wood-burner logs and require no maintenance. And the gas fires are as beautiful and warming as their wood counterparts.*

that operate efficiently using liquid petroleum gas.

Gas Log design has come a long way since the early days of the artificial log. The ceramic logs are cast from molds taken directly from real wood logs and duplicate every detail including texture, ax marks, knots and color.

The realism of the gas fire is enhanced with vermiculite and rock wool applied over a bed of sand. These embers glow realistically when the fire is burning, and add that final touch of realism.

**Note:** Always use a certified installer with gas appliances. Consult your local dealer, or refer to the appendix in the back of this book, for a dealer near you.

*Heat-N-Glo, Superior, and other suppliers offer a wide range of gas log designs that accurately mimic popular woods such as oak and birch. Your friends and family won't be able to tell the difference!*

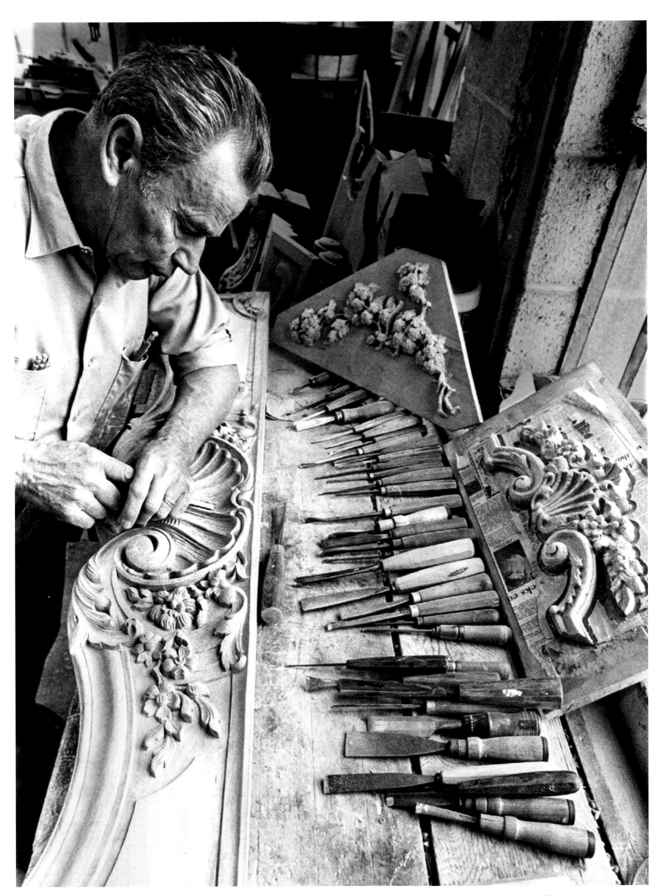

*Master Craftsman John Wohner Sr. shown carving a Louis XV frieze in 1970. This frieze is a reproduction of one found at Versailles.*

# Chapter Five

# The Mantle Masters

## Contemporary Mantel Craftsmen and Their Works

**Today's masters are preserving and improving on the old world magic of the classical mantel while creating wood and stone mantel originals that are purely stunning in their workmanship and design. Many are offering quality reproductions that are affordable, load bearing and maintenance-free.**

There are many quality artists and craftsmen producing mantels of every style in a wide range of materials from wood to cast stone. The Wohner Family, Wally Little, Stone Magic, and Brickstone represent the variety of mantel producers that provide products that are beautiful, affordable and meet safety standards and most local

*The early 1900s Wohner shop featured many heavy-duty woodworking tools. Even at that early time, machine-powered efficiency was a strategy for producing affordable carvings.*

Wohner's has created a vast array of quality designs to fit with modern installations. The finest hardwoods and finishing techniques are employed to provide a masterpiece that will last for generations.

building codes.

**Wohner's.** The Wohner Family continues a tradition of excellence.

John Wohner writes, "We are very excited to introduce our woodcarved ornaments and fireplaces which exemplify our many years of expertise in the woodworking field. Our tradition was started back in Europe in 1903 by my grandfather. His legacy was handed down through my father and was moved to the United States by him in 1956.

Our reputation was built by creating the most laborious reproduction furniture, carved panel rooms, libraries, fireplaces, carvings, etc., which decorate some of the finest homes today.

*The Wohner family success can be attributed to the close cooperation between family members. Shown here are the Wohner brothers carefully crafting a classic carving.*

Now as my sons continue as the fourth generation in the craft, we have perfected our designs to allow their use by today's craftsmen. Through the process of

*A member of the Wohner family assembles the mantel components following the carving and sanding stage.*

machine duplicating, followed by sanding to a fine detail, we offer our carvings to you economically for the first time. Architects, builders, woodworkers, designers and the like will find these carvings a great aid in creating the look which they desire on a realistic budget. Never before was it possible to find ready-made carvings in such a wide array. I

know that, as a craftsman and a designer, this marks an exciting time in the history of architecture and design.

*Every Wohner mantel design is carefully sketched and detailed prior to actual carving.*

I look forward to helping you create beautiful period and contemporary designs in all kinds of tasteful applications.

Our carvings arrive to you unfinished and pre-sanded. The majority are available in both oak and maple, and some items are available in poplar. We are constantly updating our designs and reserve the right to make changes without notice. For large and/or historical projects, we can develop carvings for your needs."

*Robert Wohner, President*

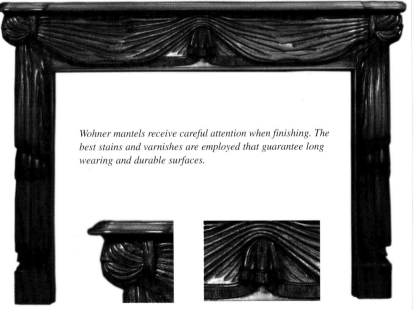

*Wohner mantels receive careful attention when finishing. The best stains and varnishes are employed that guarantee long wearing and durable surfaces.*

***Stone Magic.*** Cast stone is a dramatic addition to any home. In this section, rather than talk about the versatility, the added value, or

*This Stone Magic cast stone mantel is in a sitting area in a large family room.*

the interest behind this maintenance-free choice, we'd prefer to talk about appearance. Cast stone simply has a breathtaking effect. Stone Magic is one of the first choices in cast stone when it comes to aesthetic balance, attention to detail, superior craftsmanship and quality.

Variations of style are endless

*Each piece of stone is hand-crafted for beauty and durability. The craftsman is finishing the original keystone for the Bordeaux mantel.*

with Stone Magic – from surrounds using only one profile shape, to complex designs achieved by stacking and fitting several shapes and sizes together. Many of these designs are completely buildable by the home craftsman. You can also have one of the Stone Magic designers create a custom design and installation to precisely fit your requirements.

You'll recognize Stone Magic's quality from details like cast-in corners, matching profiles in belly bands and surrounds.

To quote Stone Magic, "Stone Magic mantels impart a graceful and lasting elegance to any home. These fireplace treatments provide a rich, old world charm without the expense. Our cast stone has the look and feel of cut limestone, but is less expensive, load-bearing, maintenance-free, and we can do intricate designs at a fraction of the cost."

Most of the designs are suitable for metal as well as masonry fireboxes. If you need help making a metal firebox work, or if you have an existing ma-

*Stone Magic's Windsor fireplace installed in a high ceiling family room. This woodburning installation adds an astounding touch of glamour to an already stunning presentation.*

*The Marquee's French influence is one of many Stone Magic floor-to-ceiling designs.*

*Stone Magic's Provence offers a range of sizes. The mantel can be purchased separately.*

special hardware required to secure the mantel and over-mantel to the wall is carefully engineered for lasting safety. The cast stone is so realistic only the most knowledgeable stone masons can tell it from the real thing.

The Provence is well-fitted to both high-efficiency gas and standard wood fireboxes and can also be incorporated with remodels.

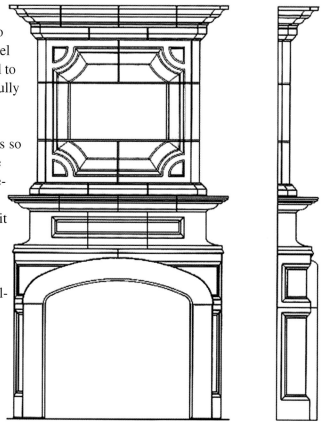

*Stone Magic's Provence is offered in the Lower Provence and Petite Provence configurations. Firebox widths run from 42" wide to 65"*

sonry firebox that does not quite work, give us a call. We specialize in both the basic fireplace installation for private homes and cabins and the grand presentation for mansions and country manors.

Every detail of your wishes will be given the attention you desire. Remember, if it is in the realm of possibilities we can probably make it work for you.

The Provence is a fine example of design and workmanship and is easily shipped and assembled. The

**The Fireside Magic Louis offering from Stone Magic is wonderfully carved with Renaissance detailing and sophistication.**

# Brickstone offers finely sculpted and hand cast murals for placement above the mantel.

### *Brickstone Studios.*

Brickstone incorporates the latest in technology with the care and elegance of Old World craftsmen. Their one piece, zero-clearance mantels are made of lightweight glass reinforced concrete which is a mixture of cement, glass fibers and water. The material is non-combustible and meets all requirements of the ASTM. They also offer NFPA Class A mantels molded using acrylic thermoplas-

tic polymers. All Brickstone mantels include mounting brackets and hardware. The standard firebox openings are 36", 42" and 48" in width.

Brickstone's creators have this to say about their work: "A medley of classic themes blends in a new and unique way to create Brickstone Studio's robust fireplace systems. Detailed to perfection, our handsome cast stone mantels form the foundation of an array of striking fireplaces. A truly distinctive touch is added with the Brickstone Limited Edition

*Brickstone murals from top include Williamsburg, Lion and the Unicorn, Lincolnshire Roses, and Timberland Chorus.*

*The Lionsgate mantel is elegant in its simplicity and is designed for installation with wood, gas or electric fireplaces. The timeless design works perfectly with traditional homes (Brickstone).*

1. Brickstone craftsmen carefully prepare the original prototype used in the mold making process. The resins used in mold making capture even the most minute details. This insures a high quality casting. The slightest flaw must be removed prior to casting to preserve the integrity of the design.

2. When preparation is completed, the prototype is coated with a high quality painted surface to preserve smoothness.

3. Following the finishing process, the surfacing material and the mold release agent are spray-applied to ensure a perfect pull-off in production. Great care is taken to create and preserve a perfect casting.

4. A Brickstone craftsman removes the mold from a solid cast hearth. The cast hearth is maintenance-free and is resistant to scuffing or cracking. All Brickstone castings are designed for generations of use.

Murals that are ideal for crowning the Brickstone mantels. Elegant top mantels are designed to frame the murals, adding a dramatic floor-to-ceiling impact. Our three dimensional murals are handcrafted by master sculptors to create vibrant works of art that are unique in every way.

Call us for a copy of our portfolio or have our artists craft a centerpiece mural to your individual requirements. Our professional design staff can develop a custom creation or work to exacting specifications."

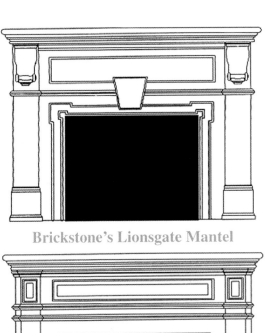

**Brickstone's Lionsgate Mantel**

**Brickstone's Williamsburg Mantel**

**Brickstone's Corinthian Mantel**

***Wally Little, Modern Master Craftsman.*** Wally has over 20 years carpentry experience from framing to custom home building. Ethics and the value of hard work and a man's word were instilled in Wally by his grandfather, Michael Pinto. Michael was a successful painting contractor and custom home builder from upstate New York. The Little Family relocation to Nevada in 1990 was driven by the building boom. Rather than become affiliated with an unknown construction company, they began their own carpentry business. Over the course of time the mantel business became the emphasis of the company.

Mantels were initially conceived with the customer as an active participating designer. In special situations they still are. However, one of Wally's basic five

designs often fulfill the needs of most customers. All new mantels are truly custom units and use Wally's basic five as a foundation only. Variations in each design are executed with specially placed corbels and rosettes.

In addition, one of Wally's greatest assets is his ability to imagine the appearance of the

final product on site and to provide valuable input to the local customer prior to ordering. He is skilled at mentally visualizing and placing the designs on paper using his highly developed sketching abilities. A skilled craftsman's appreciation of the warmth of the color of

the various woods and their required radiance in creating a

*Wally Little of Las Vegas.*

masterful mantel are skills that Wally acquired over many years of designing and building.

***Wally's first Mantel.*** A customer requested a fireplace mantel to be added during the finish carpentry phase of his home. Initial design and customer consultation took four hours.

Probably the most intense portion of the four hours was the moulding and carvings which needed to match existing decor. Working closely with the customer and witnessing his excitement was a pleasure. Later during the same year another existing customer requested a larger mantel. After extensive design work the mantel called "The Tarrytown" was developed. This large mantel, measures 72 inches between the pediments and is one of the largest Wally has built to date. Wally's mantels start at around $350. *Refer to the Appendix for Wally's full address.*

*This masterpiece, "The Tarrytown," was well received by the client and reflects the skill and workmanship Wally has developed as a craftsman. Even though all his mantels are built on the same design philosophy, no two are ever exactly alike.*

*Tile and grout designs offer a wide array of elegant interior solutions.*

# Chapter Six

# The Basic Mantel

## Wood and Tile Mantels You Can Build Easily

**Mantel construction is easy with these step-by-step building instructions. The materials are economical to purchase, and are available at most lumber yards. The parts are shaped with common tools. Each design can be completed in just a few hours.**

**Mantel design and construction begins with establishing the overall basic measurements of the installation.**

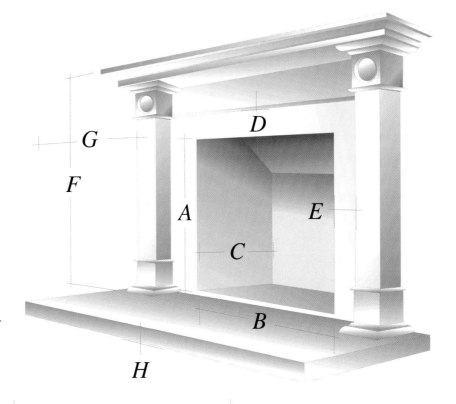

**A/B/C:** The height, width and depth of the masonry or steel firebox or insert is of first importance.

**D:** All masonry and brick installations require at least 6" of nonflammable materials surrounding the opening of the firebox. Zero-clearance fire appliances allow for close contact of flammable materials. Be sure to discuss this with a fireplace professional.

**E:** This dimension must be 12" or more when the flammable materials project out over 1-1/2" from the face of the firebox as in the case of top shelves and trim.

**F:** Most mantel designs look best with a height of 54" to 60" measured from the floor-level hearth.

**G:** All obstacles such as flammable swinging windows/draperies, open doors, light switches and cabinets must be at least 30" from the firebox opening.

**H:** The height of the hearth and the distance of its edges to the firebox opening is required for completing the dimensioning.

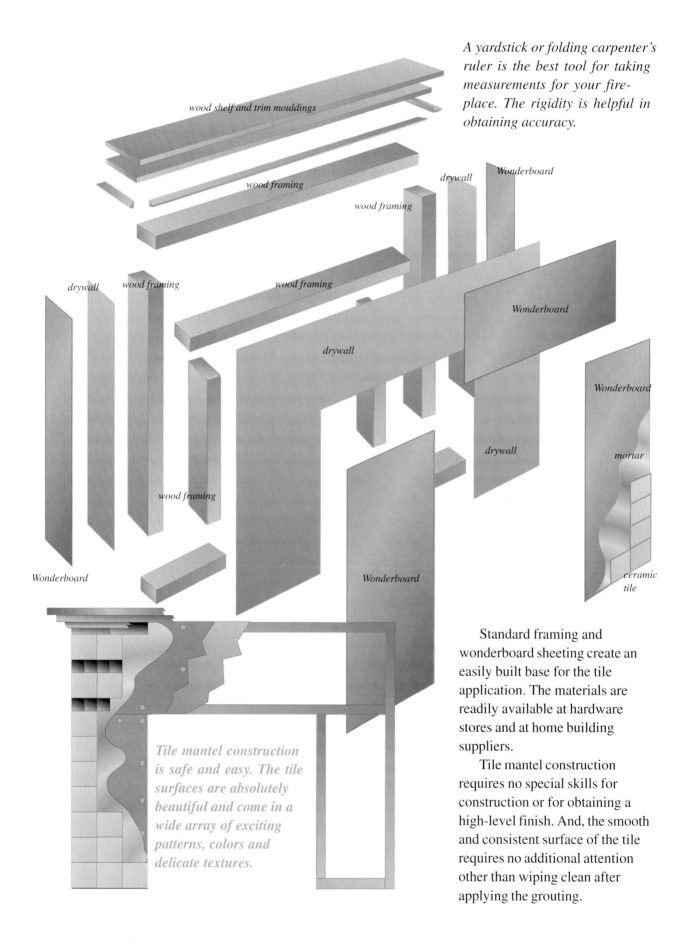

wood shelf and trim mouldings

*A yardstick or folding carpenter's ruler is the best tool for taking measurements for your fireplace. The rigidity is helpful in obtaining accuracy.*

wood framing

drywall

Wonderboard

wood framing

drywall

wood framing

wood framing

Wonderboard

drywall

drywall

Wonderboard

wood framing

mortar

Wonderboard

ceramic tile

Wonderboard

Wonderboard

*Tile mantel construction is safe and easy. The tile surfaces are absolutely beautiful and come in a wide array of exciting patterns, colors and delicate textures.*

Standard framing and wonderboard sheeting create an easily built base for the tile application. The materials are readily available at hardware stores and at home building suppliers.

Tile mantel construction requires no special skills for construction or for obtaining a high-level finish. And, the smooth and consistent surface of the tile requires no additional attention other than wiping clean after applying the grouting.

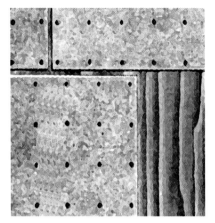

***Step 1:*** The tile mortar bed is of Wonderboard, a portland cement material. Wonderboard can be scored and snapped to size. The edges are mesh reinforced and allow for a tapeless installation.

***Step 2:*** Mark the layout for the tile with chalk or pencil using a carpenter's square. The layout lines must be at perfect right angles. Plan for cut tiles to be placed in hidden areas.

***Step 3:*** Accurately position each tile on the floor before applying mortar to determine the best layout and number of tile needed. Cut each tile that requires modification to size .

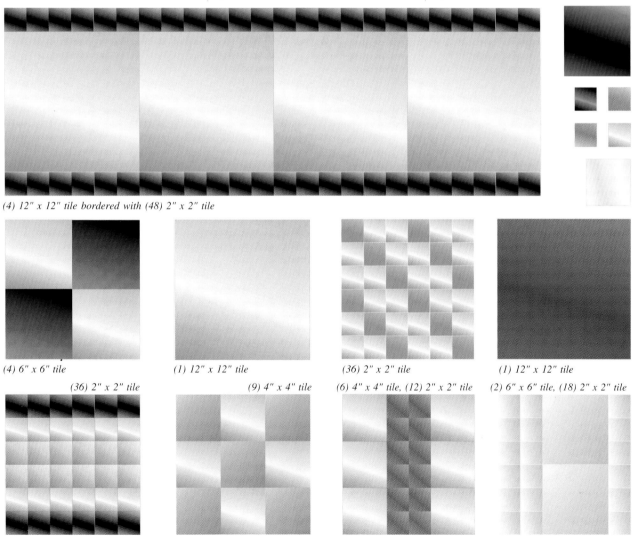

*(4) 12" x 12" tile bordered with (48) 2" x 2" tile*

*(4) 6" x 6" tile*

*(1) 12" x 12" tile*

*(36) 2" x 2" tile*

*(1) 12" x 12" tile*

*(36) 2" x 2" tile*

*(9) 4" x 4" tile*

*(6) 4" x 4" tile, (12) 2" x 2" tile*

*(2) 6" x 6" tile, (18) 2" x 2" tile*

***Step 4:*** Apply bonding materials with notched trowel held at 45 degrees. Do not spread more bonding adhesive than can be tiled in fifteen minutes. Place tile with slight twisting motion.

***Step 5:*** If needed, use tile spacers for alignment. Make final adjustments of each tile and beat into place with a block of wood and rubber mallet. Wait 48 to 72 hours before grouting.

***Step 6:*** Remove spacers from application. Using rubber float, spread grout firmly over surface and tightly into joints. Work in small sections. Smooth and finish grouting with damp towel.

*Tile mantels work well in areas where shallow-depth mantel shelves are required. This shelf is only 6" from front to back.*

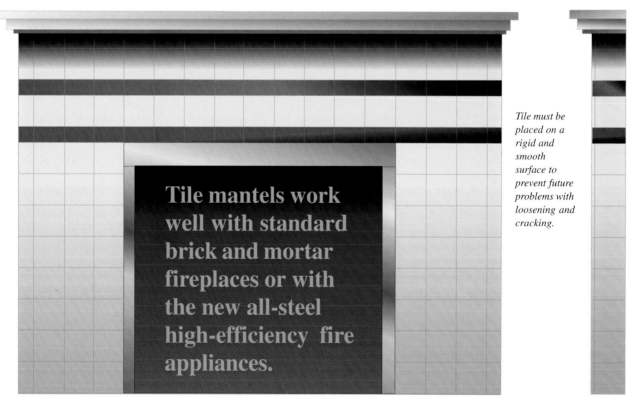

Tile mantels work well with standard brick and mortar fireplaces or with the new all-steel high-efficiency fire appliances.

*Tile must be placed on a rigid and smooth surface to prevent future problems with loosening and cracking.*

*Tile mantels are easily kept beautiful and maintenance free by sealing the grout for protection against mildews, stains, scuffing and marring.*

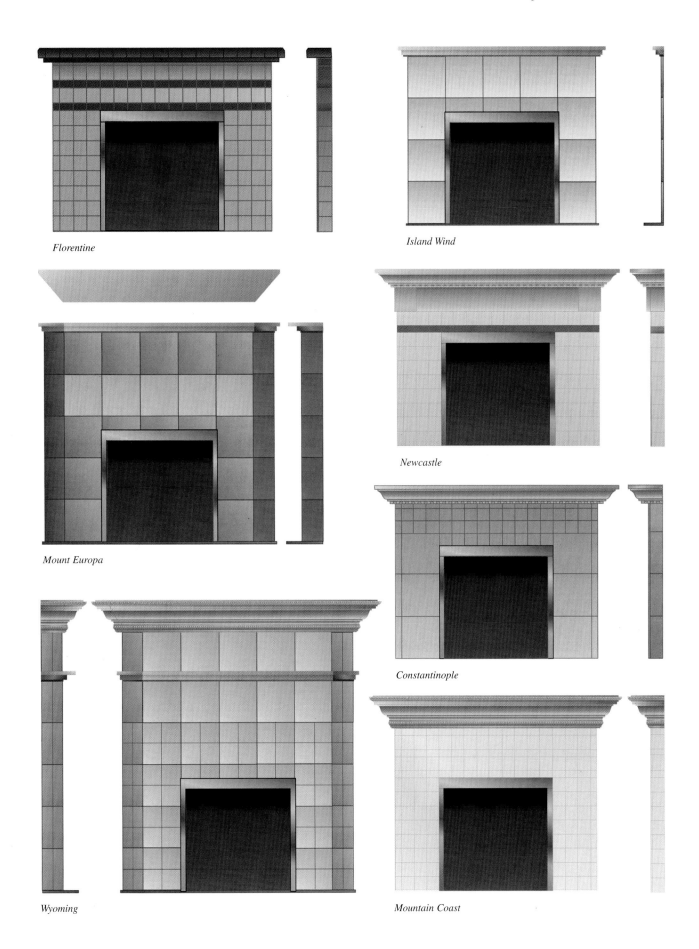

*Florentine*

*Island Wind*

*Mount Europa*

*Newcastle*

*Constantinople*

*Wyoming*

*Mountain Coast*

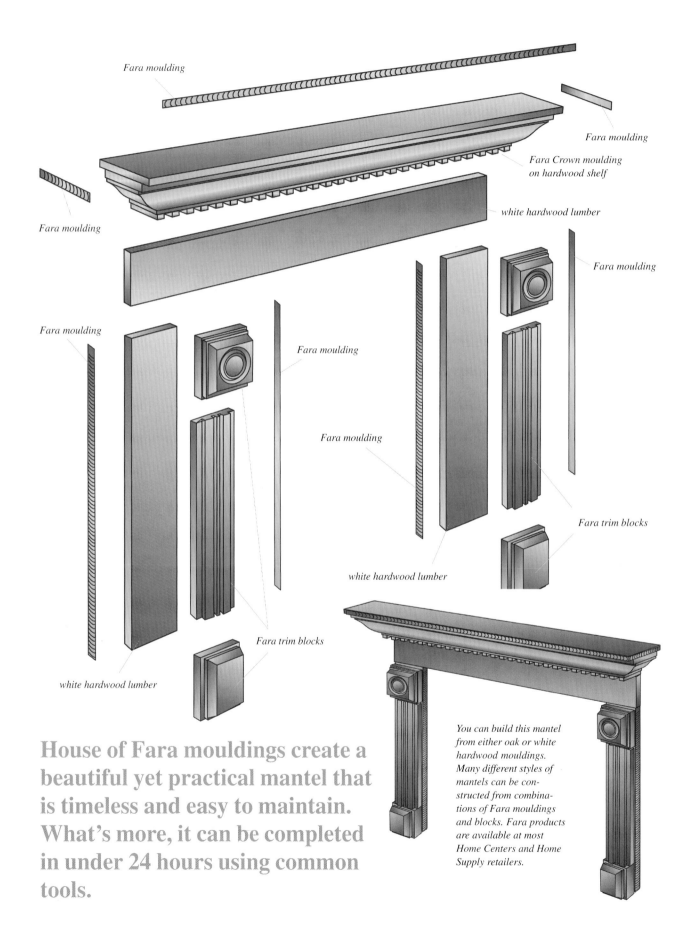

Fara moulding

Fara moulding

Fara Crown moulding
on hardwood shelf

white hardwood lumber

Fara moulding

Fara moulding

Fara moulding

Fara moulding

Fara moulding

Fara moulding

Fara trim blocks

white hardwood lumber

Fara trim blocks

white hardwood lumber

**House of Fara mouldings create a beautiful yet practical mantel that is timeless and easy to maintain. What's more, it can be completed in under 24 hours using common tools.**

*You can build this mantel from either oak or white hardwood mouldings. Many different styles of mantels can be constructed from combinations of Fara mouldings and blocks. Fara products are available at most Home Centers and Home Supply retailers.*

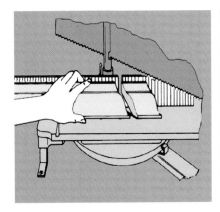 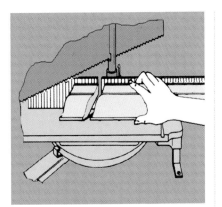 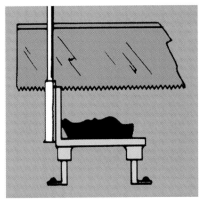

***Step 1:*** Determine the length of the top shelf. Position the crown moulding front piece in a mitre box with the bottom of the moulding tightly against the fence. Set the saw angle at 45 degrees to left and slowly saw through the moulding.

***Step 2:*** Carefully measure and cut the opposite end of the crown moulding front piece using the same technique but changing the mitre box angle exactly to 45 degrees to the right. Lay the moulding side piece in the mitre box and cut.

***Step 3:*** The left and right end side piece angles are sawn using the same methods as employed when cutting the front piece angles. The right angled cuts are completed with the moulding lying flat on the saw bed and held tightly with the free hand.

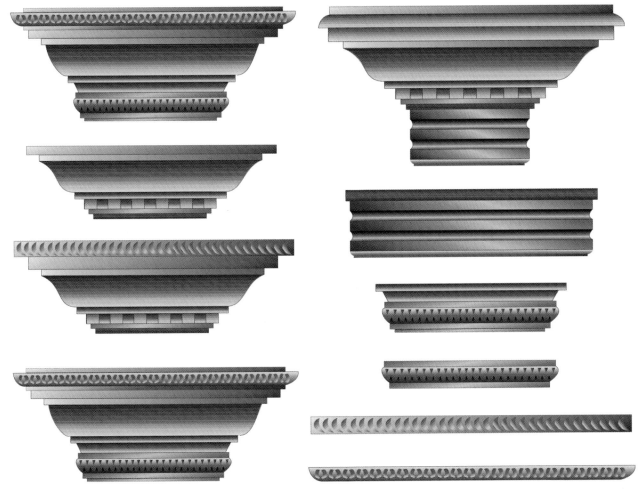

*These classically dramatic crowns were each entirely created with House of Fara components.*

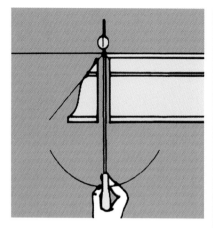

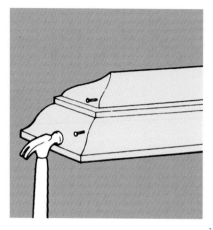

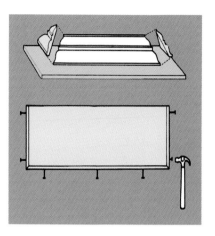

**Step 4:** The mitre saw is easily adjusted to create the right-angled and the 45-degree cuts. The two left and right end pieces have both types of angles. The front piece has the 45-degree angles cut into both ends.

**Step 5:** Assemble all pieces using stainable wood glue and finishing nails to create the complete crown moulding assembly. Countersink the nail heads and fill the holes with a matching wood putty.

**Step 6:** The crown moulding shelf is edge-finished with House of Fara strip mouldings. Fara offers several designs of embossed mouldings that can be glued to the edge of exposed lumber to create a carved look.

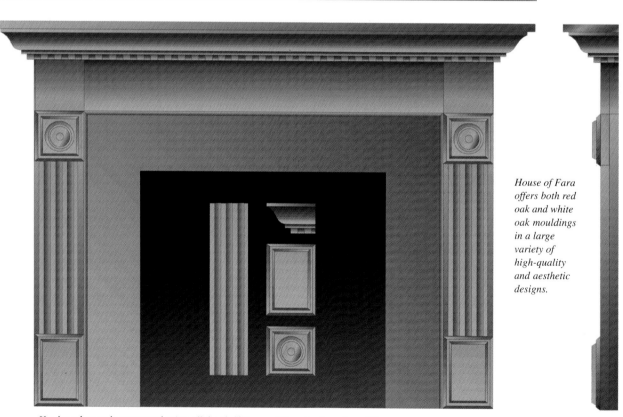

*House of Fara offers both red oak and white oak mouldings in a large variety of high-quality and aesthetic designs.*

*Hardwood mantel constructed using off-the-shelf House of Fara hardwood mouldings.*

*Applique Mantel with Superior Fireplace Company High Efficiency Insert.*

*Cherrywood Fireplace Mantel with Superior Fireplace Company refractory brick and steel fireplace.*

# Chapter Seven

# Mantels Portfolio

## Exploded Views and Illustrations of Original Designs

**Mantel planning and design are easy using these informative overviews. Suggested materials are readily available at most lumber yards at affordable prices. Parts are shaped with common tools. The designs are easily completed in your spare time.**

***Important design note:*** When planning your original fireplace mantel design, carefully coordinate the style of the mantel you design and build with the type of firebox you fit it with. The zero-clearance gas and wood fireplaces allow the mantel to fit right against the firebox opening. Standard steel open-fire fireplaces and the classic brick and mortar units must be allowed clearance for combustible materials. On standard fireplaces that translates to at least six inches of space between the firebox front edge and the combustible mantel materials that fit close to it.

Laguna, pg. 60

Woodside, pg. 61

Sherwood, pg. 62

Cherrybeane, pg. 63

Cherrywood, pg. 64

Oak Manor, pg. 65

Mohawk, pg. 66

Cherrytree, pg. 67

Temple, pg. 68

Timberview, pg. 69

Fawn Manor, pg. 70

Palacian, pg. 71

Celecia, pg. 72

Pharoah, pg. 73

Psychodelic, pg. 74

Afrikan, pg. 75

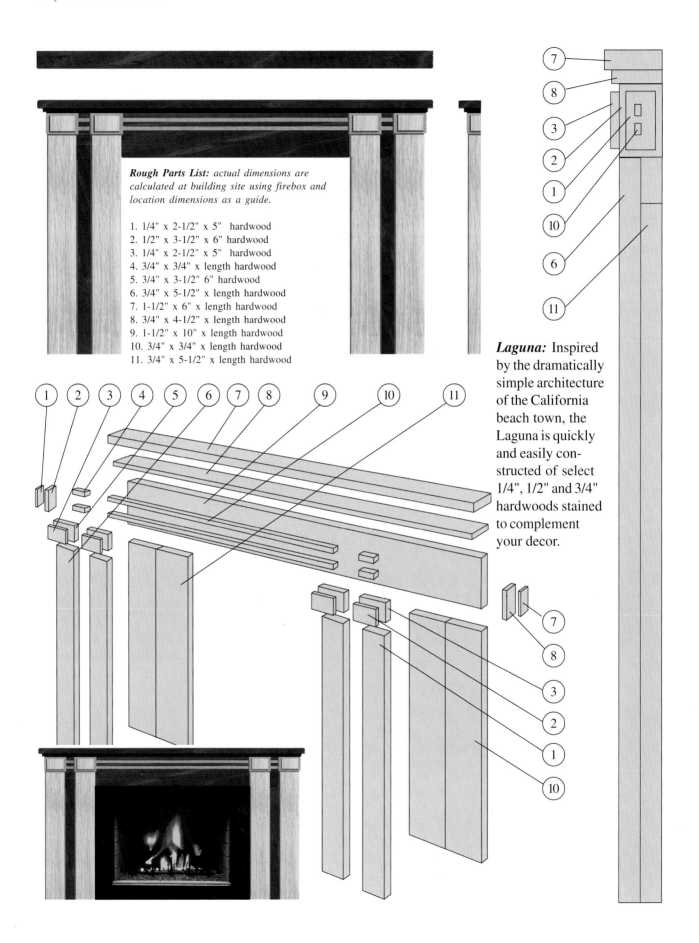

**Rough Parts List:** *actual dimensions are calculated at building site using firebox and location dimensions as a guide.*

1. 1/4" x 2-1/2" x 5"  hardwood
2. 1/2" x 3-1/2" x 6" hardwood
3. 1/4" x 2-1/2" x 5"  hardwood
4. 3/4" x 3/4" x length hardwood
5. 3/4" x 3-1/2" 6" hardwood
6. 3/4" x 5-1/2" x length hardwood
7. 1-1/2" x 6" x length hardwood
8. 3/4" x 4-1/2" x length hardwood
9. 1-1/2" x 10" x length hardwood
10. 3/4" x 3/4" x length hardwood
11. 3/4" x 5-1/2" x length hardwood

***Laguna:*** Inspired by the dramatically simple architecture of the California beach town, the Laguna is quickly and easily constructed of select 1/4", 1/2" and 3/4" hardwoods stained to complement your decor.

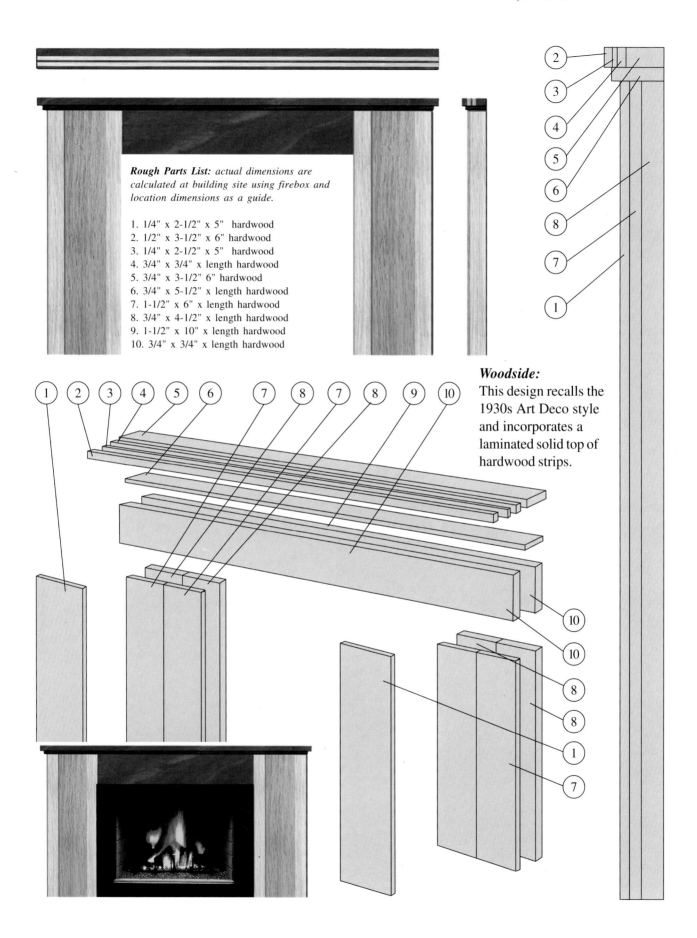

**Rough Parts List:** *actual dimensions are calculated at building site using firebox and location dimensions as a guide.*

1. 1/4" x 2-1/2" x 5" hardwood
2. 1/2" x 3-1/2" x 6" hardwood
3. 1/4" x 2-1/2" x 5" hardwood
4. 3/4" x 3/4" x length hardwood
5. 3/4" x 3-1/2" 6" hardwood
6. 3/4" x 5-1/2" x length hardwood
7. 1-1/2" x 6" x length hardwood
8. 3/4" x 4-1/2" x length hardwood
9. 1-1/2" x 10" x length hardwood
10. 3/4" x 3/4" x length hardwood

***Woodside:***

This design recalls the 1930s Art Deco style and incorporates a laminated solid top of hardwood strips.

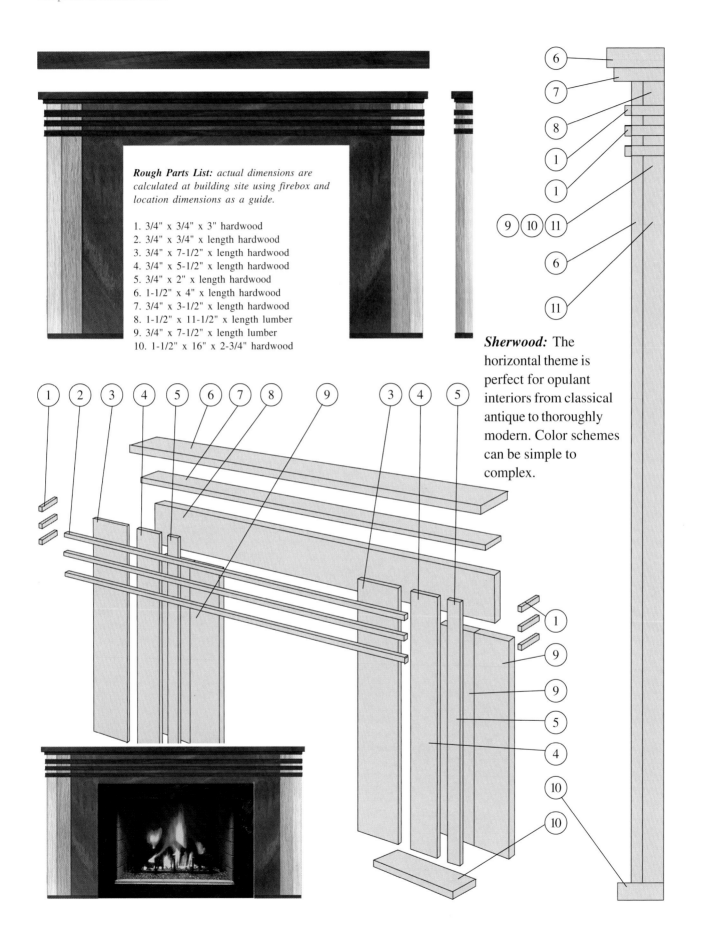

**Rough Parts List:** *actual dimensions are calculated at building site using firebox and location dimensions as a guide.*

1. 3/4" x 3/4" x 3" hardwood
2. 3/4" x 3/4" x length hardwood
3. 3/4" x 7-1/2" x length hardwood
4. 3/4" x 5-1/2" x length hardwood
5. 3/4" x 2" x length hardwood
6. 1-1/2" x 4" x length hardwood
7. 3/4" x 3-1/2" x length hardwood
8. 1-1/2" x 11-1/2" x length lumber
9. 3/4" x 7-1/2" x length lumber
10. 1-1/2" x 16" x 2-3/4" hardwood

**Sherwood:** The horizontal theme is perfect for opulant interiors from classical antique to thoroughly modern. Color schemes can be simple to complex.

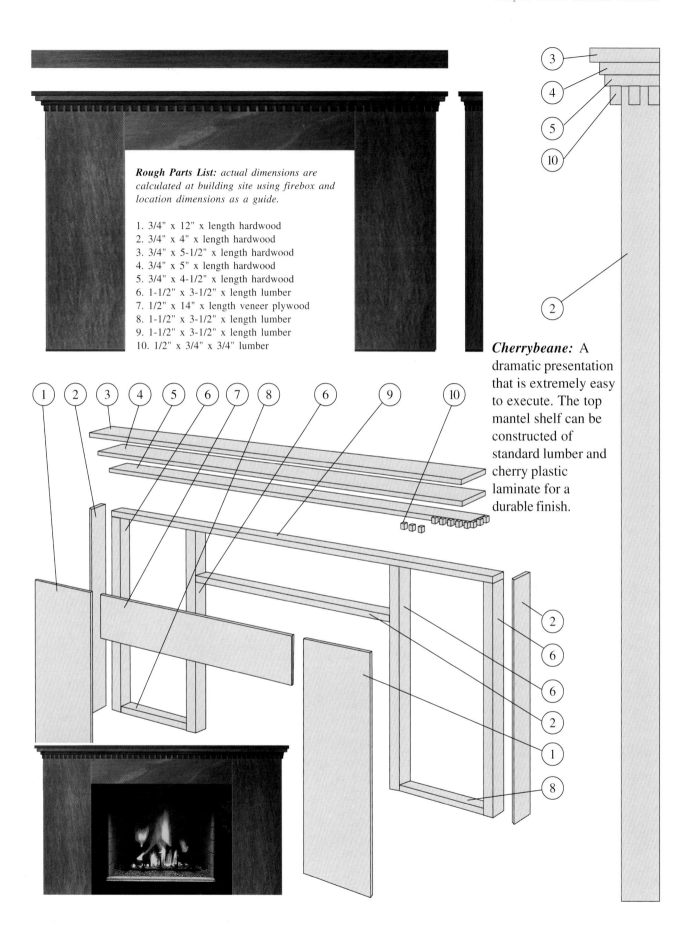

**Rough Parts List:** *actual dimensions are calculated at building site using firebox and location dimensions as a guide.*

1. 3/4" x 12" x length hardwood
2. 3/4" x 4" x length hardwood
3. 3/4" x 5-1/2" x length hardwood
4. 3/4" x 5" x length hardwood
5. 3/4" x 4-1/2" x length hardwood
6. 1-1/2" x 3-1/2" x length lumber
7. 1/2" x 14" x length veneer plywood
8. 1-1/2" x 3-1/2" x length lumber
9. 1-1/2" x 3-1/2" x length lumber
10. 1/2" x 3/4" x 3/4" lumber

*Cherrybeane:* A dramatic presentation that is extremely easy to execute. The top mantel shelf can be constructed of standard lumber and cherry plastic laminate for a durable finish.

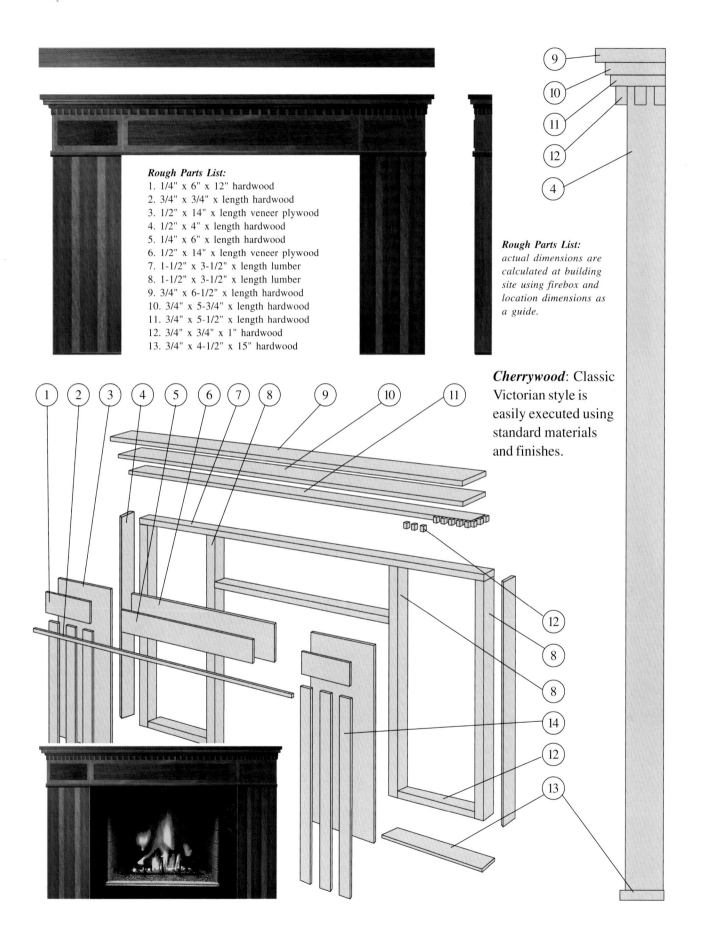

**Rough Parts List:**
1. 1/4" x 6" x 12" hardwood
2. 3/4" x 3/4" x length hardwood
3. 1/2" x 14" x length veneer plywood
4. 1/2" x 4" x length hardwood
5. 1/4" x 6" x length hardwood
6. 1/2" x 14" x length veneer plywood
7. 1-1/2" x 3-1/2" x length lumber
8. 1-1/2" x 3-1/2" x length lumber
9. 3/4" x 6-1/2" x length hardwood
10. 3/4" x 5-3/4" x length hardwood
11. 3/4" x 5-1/2" x length hardwood
12. 3/4" x 3/4" x 1" hardwood
13. 3/4" x 4-1/2" x 15" hardwood

**Rough Parts List:**
*actual dimensions are calculated at building site using firebox and location dimensions as a guide.*

**Cherrywood**: Classic Victorian style is easily executed using standard materials and finishes.

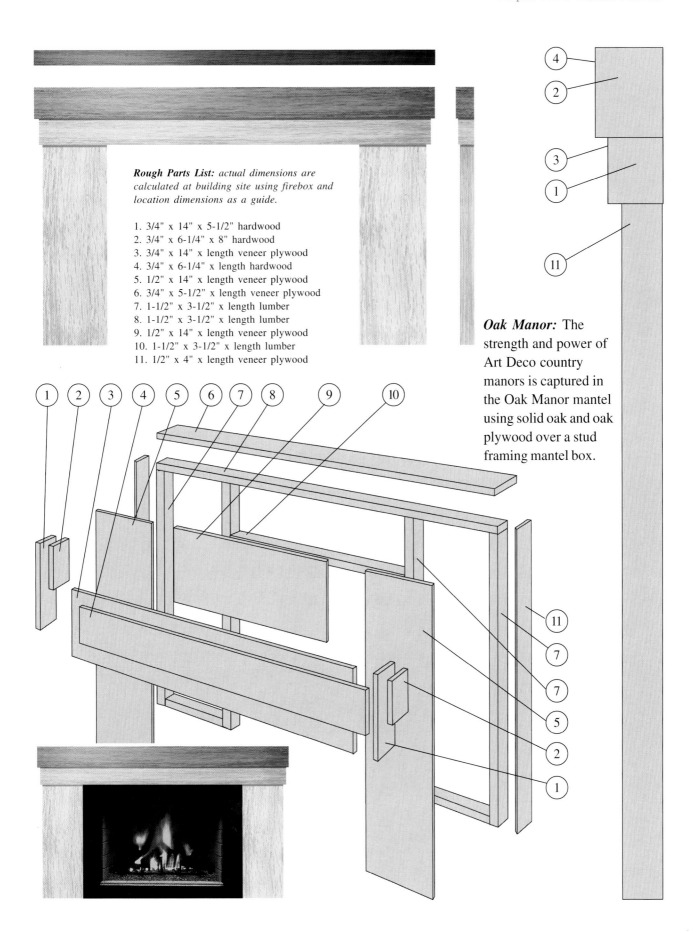

*Rough Parts List:* actual dimensions are calculated at building site using firebox and location dimensions as a guide.

1. 3/4" x 14" x 5-1/2" hardwood
2. 3/4" x 6-1/4" x 8" hardwood
3. 3/4" x 14" x length veneer plywood
4. 3/4" x 6-1/4" x length hardwood
5. 1/2" x 14" x length veneer plywood
6. 3/4" x 5-1/2" x length veneer plywood
7. 1-1/2" x 3-1/2" x length lumber
8. 1-1/2" x 3-1/2" x length lumber
9. 1/2" x 14" x length veneer plywood
10. 1-1/2" x 3-1/2" x length lumber
11. 1/2" x 4" x length veneer plywood

*Oak Manor:* The strength and power of Art Deco country manors is captured in the Oak Manor mantel using solid oak and oak plywood over a stud framing mantel box.

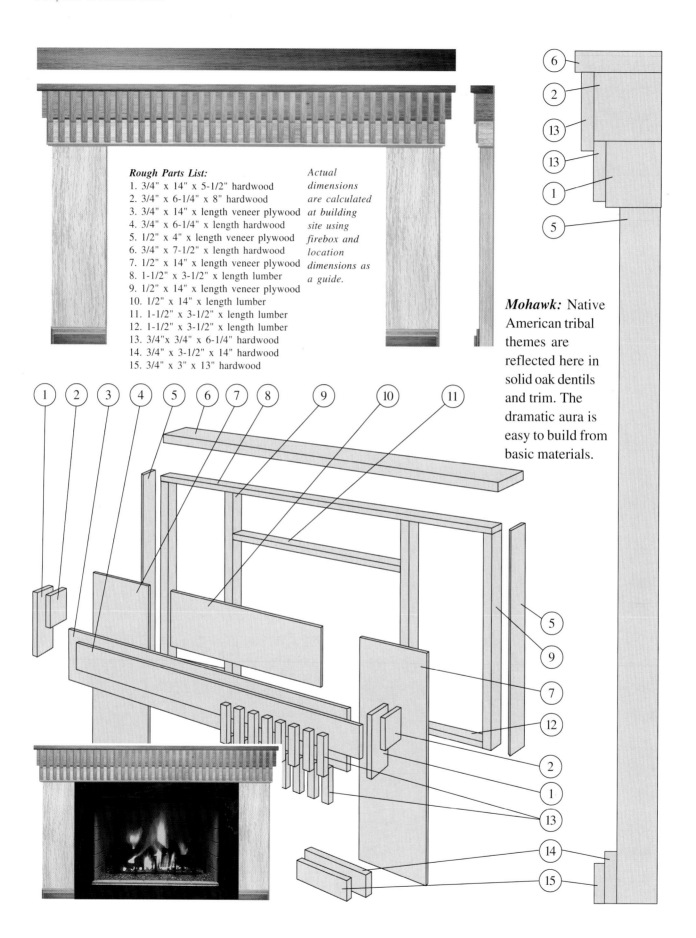

***Rough Parts List:***
1. 3/4" x 14" x 5-1/2" hardwood
2. 3/4" x 6-1/4" x 8" hardwood
3. 3/4" x 14" x length veneer plywood
4. 3/4" x 6-1/4" x length hardwood
5. 1/2" x 4" x length veneer plywood
6. 3/4" x 7-1/2" x length hardwood
7. 1/2" x 14" x length veneer plywood
8. 1-1/2" x 3-1/2" x length lumber
9. 1/2" x 14" x length veneer plywood
10. 1/2" x 14" x length lumber
11. 1-1/2" x 3-1/2" x length lumber
12. 1-1/2" x 3-1/2" x length lumber
13. 3/4"x 3/4" x 6-1/4" hardwood
14. 3/4" x 3-1/2" x 14" hardwood
15. 3/4" x 3" x 13" hardwood

*Actual dimensions are calculated at building site using firebox and location dimensions as a guide.*

***Mohawk:*** Native American tribal themes are reflected here in solid oak dentils and trim. The dramatic aura is easy to build from basic materials.

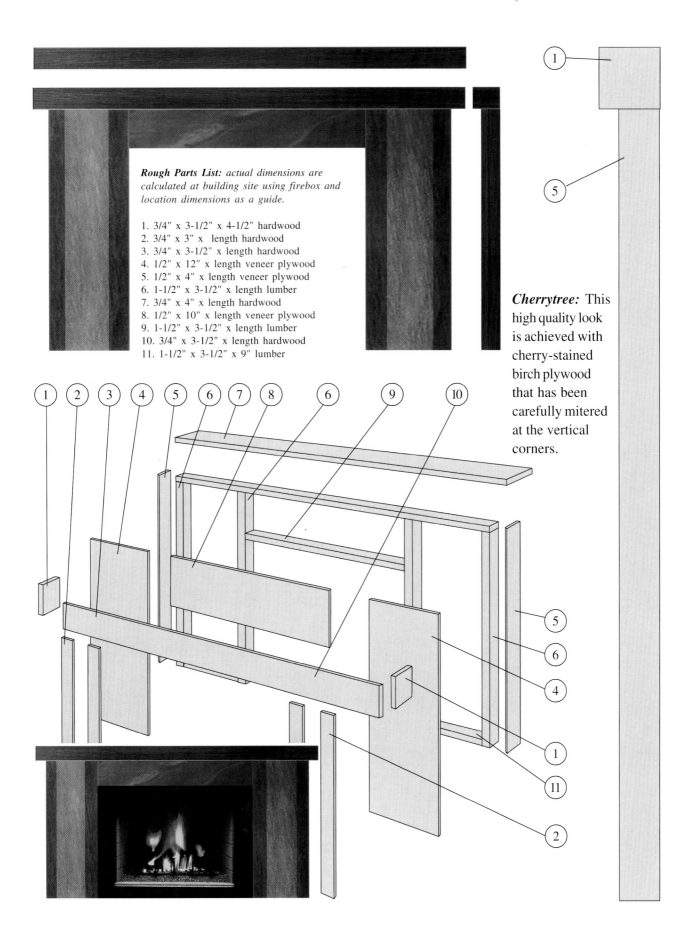

**Rough Parts List:** *actual dimensions are calculated at building site using firebox and location dimensions as a guide.*

1. 3/4" x 3-1/2" x 4-1/2" hardwood
2. 3/4" x 3" x  length hardwood
3. 3/4" x 3-1/2" x length hardwood
4. 1/2" x 12" x length veneer plywood
5. 1/2" x 4" x length veneer plywood
6. 1-1/2" x 3-1/2" x length lumber
7. 3/4" x 4" x length hardwood
8. 1/2" x 10" x length veneer plywood
9. 1-1/2" x 3-1/2" x length lumber
10. 3/4" x 3-1/2" x length hardwood
11. 1-1/2" x 3-1/2" x 9" lumber

***Cherrytree:*** This high quality look is achieved with cherry-stained birch plywood that has been carefully mitered at the vertical corners.

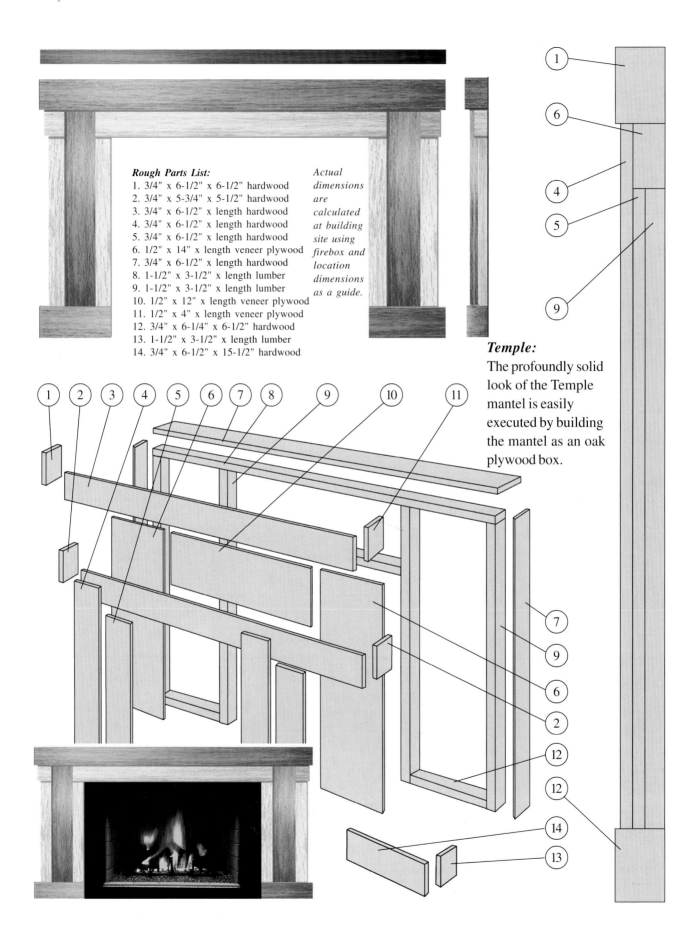

**Rough Parts List:**
1. 3/4" x 6-1/2" x 6-1/2" hardwood
2. 3/4" x 5-3/4" x 5-1/2" hardwood
3. 3/4" x 6-1/2" x length hardwood
4. 3/4" x 6-1/2" x length hardwood
5. 3/4" x 6-1/2" x length hardwood
6. 1/2" x 14" x length veneer plywood
7. 3/4" x 6-1/2" x length hardwood
8. 1-1/2" x 3-1/2" x length lumber
9. 1-1/2" x 3-1/2" x length lumber
10. 1/2" x 12" x length veneer plywood
11. 1/2" x 4" x length veneer plywood
12. 3/4" x 6-1/4" x 6-1/2" hardwood
13. 1-1/2" x 3-1/2" x length lumber
14. 3/4" x 6-1/2" x 15-1/2" hardwood

*Actual dimensions are calculated at building site using firebox and location dimensions as a guide.*

## Temple:

The profoundly solid look of the Temple mantel is easily executed by building the mantel as an oak plywood box.

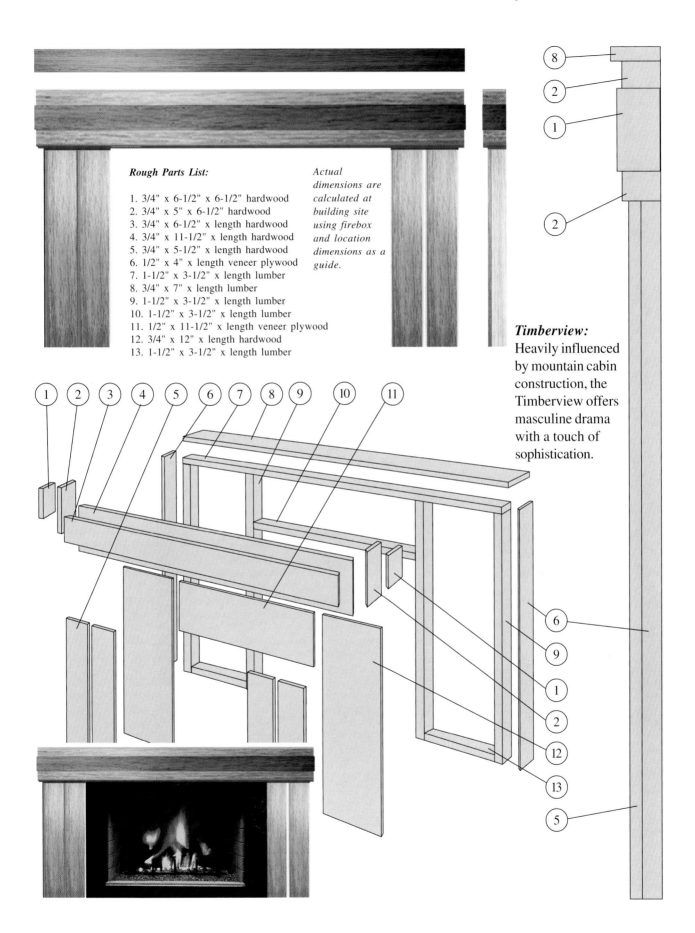

***Rough Parts List:***

1. 3/4" x 6-1/2" x 6-1/2" hardwood
2. 3/4" x 5" x 6-1/2" hardwood
3. 3/4" x 6-1/2" x length hardwood
4. 3/4" x 11-1/2" x length hardwood
5. 3/4" x 5-1/2" x length hardwood
6. 1/2" x 4" x length veneer plywood
7. 1-1/2" x 3-1/2" x length lumber
8. 3/4" x 7" x length lumber
9. 1-1/2" x 3-1/2" x length lumber
10. 1-1/2" x 3-1/2" x length lumber
11. 1/2" x 11-1/2" x length veneer plywood
12. 3/4" x 12" x length hardwood
13. 1-1/2" x 3-1/2" x length lumber

*Actual dimensions are calculated at building site using firebox and location dimensions as a guide.*

***Timberview:***
Heavily influenced by mountain cabin construction, the Timberview offers masculine drama with a touch of sophistication.

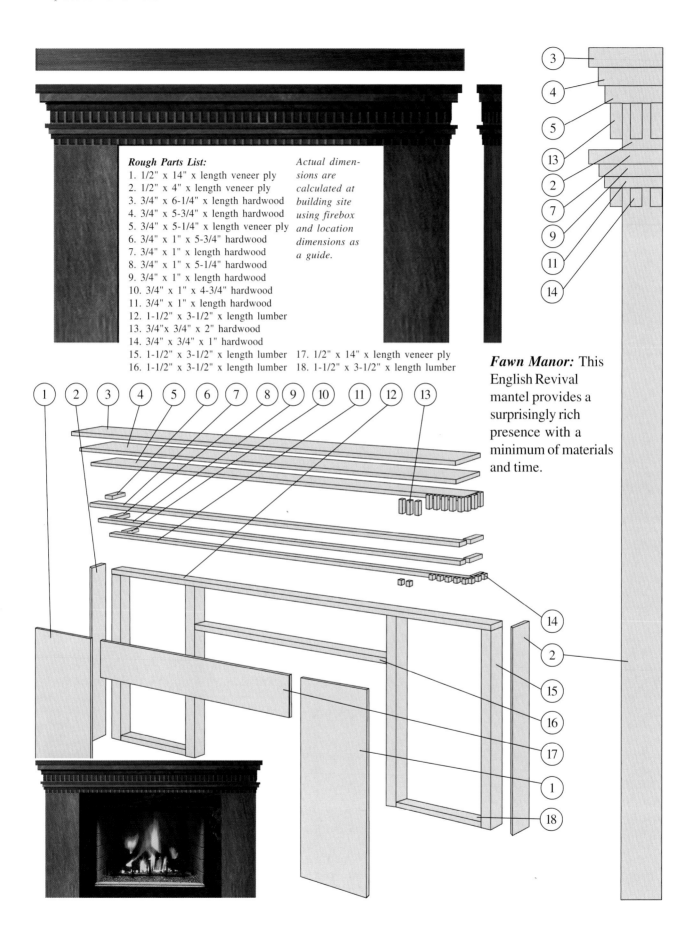

**Rough Parts List:**
1. 1/2" x 14" x length veneer ply
2. 1/2" x 4" x length veneer ply
3. 3/4" x 6-1/4" x length hardwood
4. 3/4" x 5-3/4" x length hardwood
5. 3/4" x 5-1/4" x length veneer ply
6. 3/4" x 1" x 5-3/4" hardwood
7. 3/4" x 1" x length hardwood
8. 3/4" x 1" x 5-1/4" hardwood
9. 3/4" x 1" x length hardwood
10. 3/4" x 1" x 4-3/4" hardwood
11. 3/4" x 1" x length hardwood
12. 1-1/2" x 3-1/2" x length lumber
13. 3/4" x 3/4" x 2" hardwood
14. 3/4" x 3/4" x 1" hardwood
15. 1-1/2" x 3-1/2" x length lumber
16. 1-1/2" x 3-1/2" x length lumber
17. 1/2" x 14" x length veneer ply
18. 1-1/2" x 3-1/2" x length lumber

*Actual dimensions are calculated at building site using firebox and location dimensions as a guide.*

***Fawn Manor:*** This English Revival mantel provides a surprisingly rich presence with a minimum of materials and time.

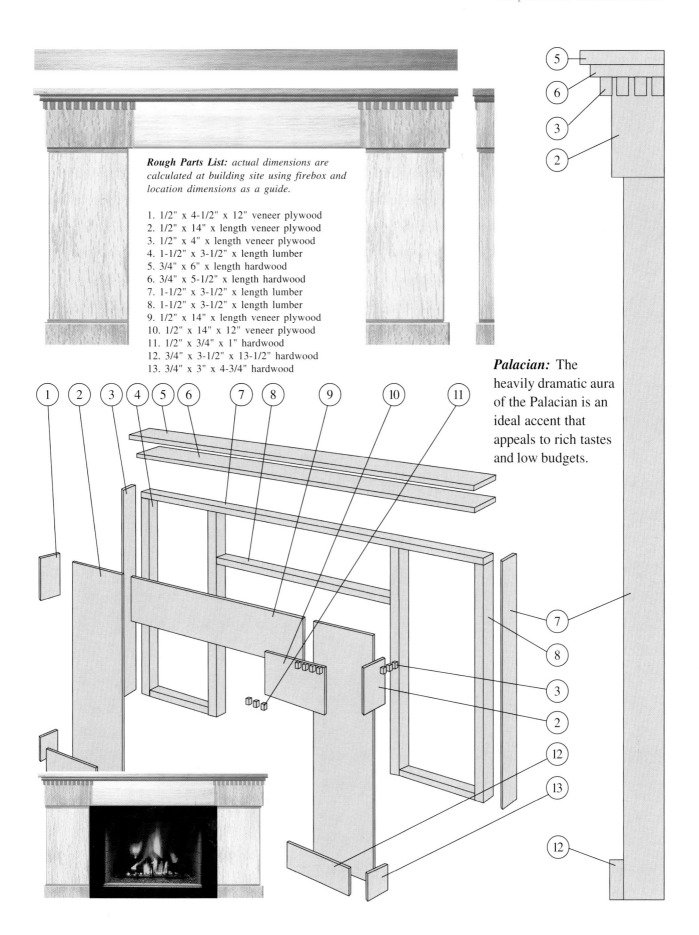

*Rough Parts List:* actual dimensions are calculated at building site using firebox and location dimensions as a guide.

1. 1/2" x 4-1/2" x 12" veneer plywood
2. 1/2" x 14" x length veneer plywood
3. 1/2" x 4" x length veneer plywood
4. 1-1/2" x 3-1/2" x length lumber
5. 3/4" x 6" x length hardwood
6. 3/4" x 5-1/2" x length hardwood
7. 1-1/2" x 3-1/2" x length lumber
8. 1-1/2" x 3-1/2" x length lumber
9. 1/2" x 14" x length veneer plywood
10. 1/2" x 14" x 12" veneer plywood
11. 1/2" x 3/4" x 1" hardwood
12. 3/4" x 3-1/2" x 13-1/2" hardwood
13. 3/4" x 3" x 4-3/4" hardwood

*Palacian:* The heavily dramatic aura of the Palacian is an ideal accent that appeals to rich tastes and low budgets.

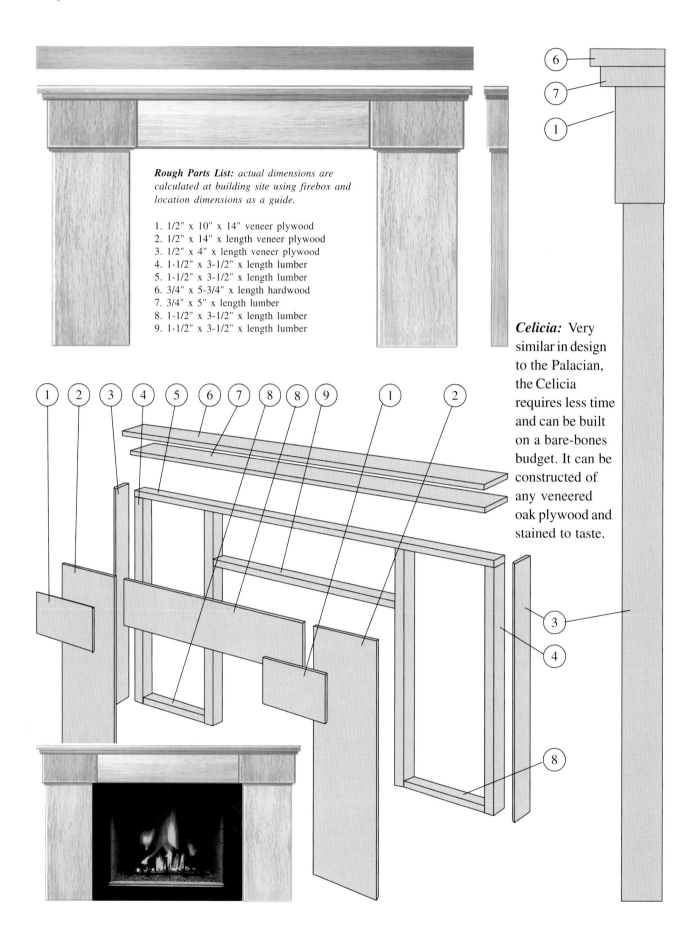

**Rough Parts List:** *actual dimensions are calculated at building site using firebox and location dimensions as a guide.*

1. 1/2" x 10" x 14" veneer plywood
2. 1/2" x 14" x length veneer plywood
3. 1/2" x 4" x length veneer plywood
4. 1-1/2" x 3-1/2" x length lumber
5. 1-1/2" x 3-1/2" x length lumber
6. 3/4" x 5-3/4" x length hardwood
7. 3/4" x 5" x length lumber
8. 1-1/2" x 3-1/2" x length lumber
9. 1-1/2" x 3-1/2" x length lumber

*Celicia:* Very similar in design to the Palacian, the Celicia requires less time and can be built on a bare-bones budget. It can be constructed of any veneered oak plywood and stained to taste.

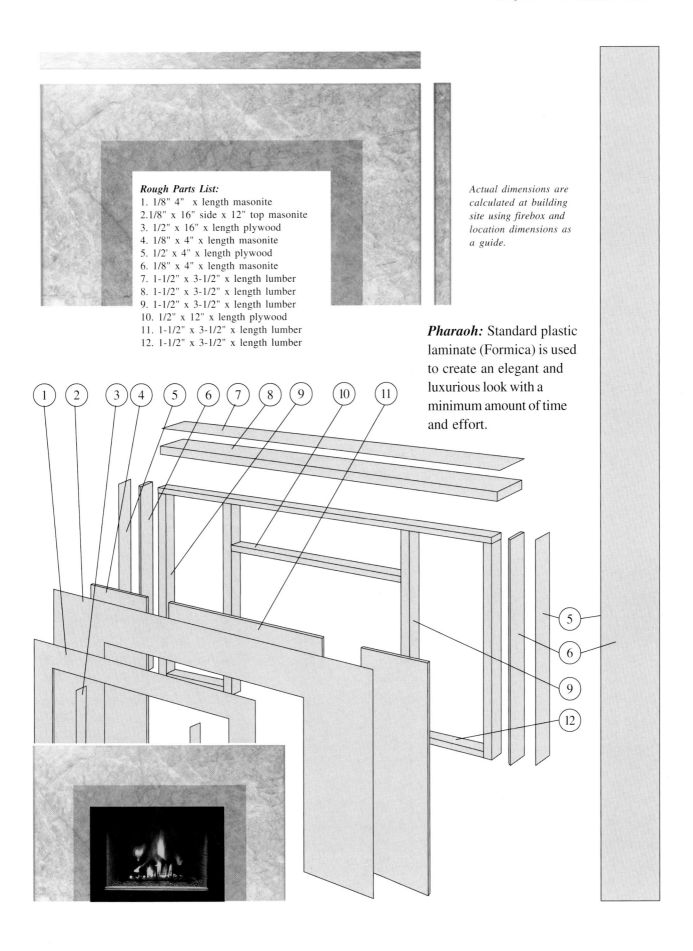

**Rough Parts List:**
1. 1/8" 4"  x length masonite
2. 1/8" x 16" side x 12" top masonite
3. 1/2" x 16" x length plywood
4. 1/8" x 4" x length masonite
5. 1/2' x 4" x length plywood
6. 1/8" x 4" x length masonite
7. 1-1/2" x 3-1/2" x length lumber
8. 1-1/2" x 3-1/2" x length lumber
9. 1-1/2" x 3-1/2" x length lumber
10. 1/2" x 12" x length plywood
11. 1-1/2" x 3-1/2" x length lumber
12. 1-1/2" x 3-1/2" x length lumber

*Actual dimensions are calculated at building site using firebox and location dimensions as a guide.*

***Pharaoh:*** Standard plastic laminate (Formica) is used to create an elegant and luxurious look with a minimum amount of time and effort.

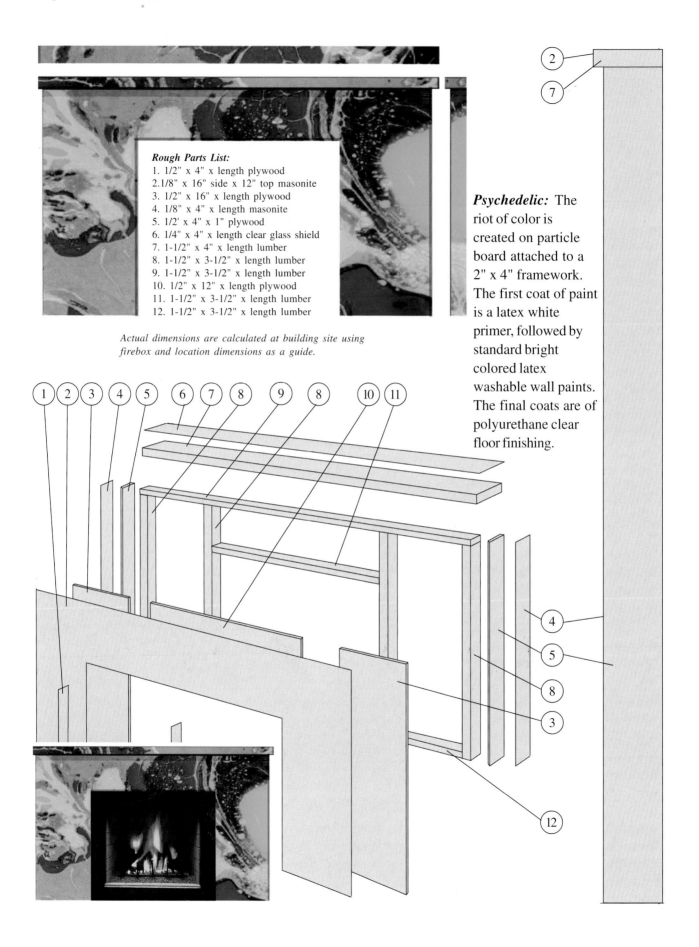

**Rough Parts List:**
1. 1/2" x 4" x length plywood
2. 1/8" x 16" side x 12" top masonite
3. 1/2" x 16" x length plywood
4. 1/8" x 4" x length masonite
5. 1/2' x 4" x 1" plywood
6. 1/4" x 4" x length clear glass shield
7. 1-1/2" x 4" x length lumber
8. 1-1/2" x 3-1/2" x length lumber
9. 1-1/2" x 3-1/2" x length lumber
10. 1/2" x 12" x length plywood
11. 1-1/2" x 3-1/2" x length lumber
12. 1-1/2" x 3-1/2" x length lumber

*Actual dimensions are calculated at building site using firebox and location dimensions as a guide.*

***Psychedelic:*** The riot of color is created on particle board attached to a 2" x 4" framework. The first coat of paint is a latex white primer, followed by standard bright colored latex washable wall paints. The final coats are of polyurethane clear floor finishing.

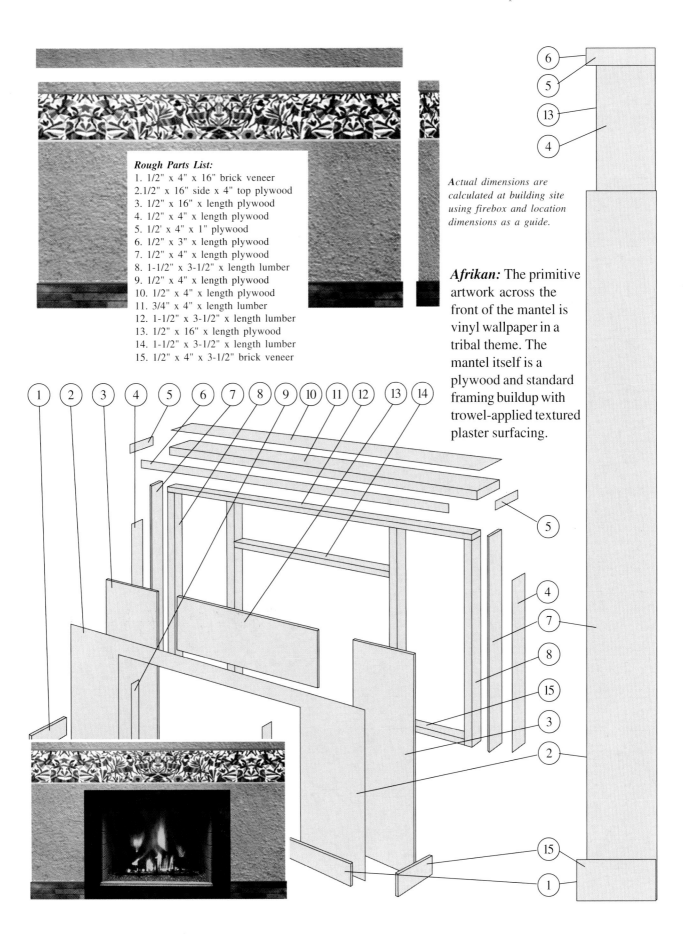

**Rough Parts List:**
1. 1/2" x 4" x 16" brick veneer
2. 1/2" x 16" side x 4" top plywood
3. 1/2" x 16" x length plywood
4. 1/2" x 4" x length plywood
5. 1/2' x 4" x 1" plywood
6. 1/2" x 3" x length plywood
7. 1/2" x 4" x length plywood
8. 1-1/2" x 3-1/2" x length lumber
9. 1/2" x 4" x length plywood
10. 1/2" x 4" x length plywood
11. 3/4" x 4" x length lumber
12. 1-1/2" x 3-1/2" x length lumber
13. 1/2" x 16" x length plywood
14. 1-1/2" x 3-1/2" x length lumber
15. 1/2" x 4" x 3-1/2" brick veneer

*Actual dimensions are calculated at building site using firebox and location dimensions as a guide.*

**Afrikan:** The primitive artwork across the front of the mantel is vinyl wallpaper in a tribal theme. The mantel itself is a plywood and standard framing buildup with trowel-applied textured plaster surfacing.

*Superior Fireplace Company.*

# Chapter Eight

# Idea Gallery

## Photos of Existing Fireplace Installations

**Mantels are an integral part of a home's ambiance. We've put together this assortment of existing photos that cover a wide range of tastes and styles. We hope you enjoy reviewing them as much as we enjoyed compiling the collection.**

Doing the research for your own fireplace mantel and then managing the installation yourself is a real pleasure, and whether you build or buy, the results are happily rewarding. There is nothing quite as satisfying as personally creating an addition to your home or special living space that you and your loved ones can enjoy for years to come.

What's more, adding a new fireplace to your home is a surefire way to increase its value.

When planning your installation, take advantage of resources available at local fireplace dealers. Their help is priceless.

# Fireplace Dealers and Suppliers

## United States and Canada

**Local dealers are your best bet for obtaining quality assistance when planning for a fireplace mantel or a complete installation. Using their expertise helps create a project that is safe, economical and an improvement to the quality and value of your home** *(suppliers on page 89).*

*Dealers in Alabama – Georgia*

**LITTLE INSULATION INC.**
3755 Hwy 431 North
Phenix City, Alabama 36867
(334) 297-1457
(334) 298-1547 (Fax)

**DIAMOND HEATING COMFORT SYSTEMS INC.**
5406 Lake Otis Parkway
Anchorage, Alaska 99507
(907) 561-3490
(907) 561-9260 (Fax)

**MOORE HEATING & AIR COND. INC.**
510 E. International Airport Rd.
Anchorage, Alaska 99518
(907) 561-1500
(800) 478-6673
(907) 561-9260 (Fax)

**GOLDEN FLAME DISTRIBUTING, INC.**
15855 N. Greenway-Hayden Loop
Suite 170
Scottsdale, Arizona 85260
(602) 948-9919
(800) 820-2373

**WESTERN LUMBER**
3911 North Hwy Dr.
Tucson, Arizona 85705
(520) 292-0801

**STAN GREER MILL WORKS**
5930 S. Hwy. 92
Sierra Vista, Arizona 85636
(520) 378-9311

Currently there are no Authorized Dealers listed in the state of Arkansas. Please consult a state near you or contact Heat-N-Glo at 1-888-743-2887 for additional dealers in your vicinity.

**THE FIREPLACE COMPANY**
3590 Sunrise Blvd.
Rancho Cordova, California 95742
(916) 635-9988
(916) 635-9913 (Fax)

**CALIFORNIA WINDOW AND FIREPLACE OUTLET**
2090 Winchester Blvd.
Campbell, California 95008
(408) 379-9930 (408) 379-1471 (Fax)

**DON LANCE HEATING & FIREPLACE OUTLET**
2227 James Ave. Unit B
South Lake Tahoe, California 96150
(530) 542-2840

**CENTRAL DISTRIBUTING**
5561 W. San Madele
Fresno, California 93722
(209) 276-1500
(209) 276-7878

**ABERCROMBIE & CO. STOVES & STUFF**
13338 B Colfax Hwy
Grass Valley, California 95945
(916) 273-5400

**ENERGY HOUSE**
635 Sanborn
Salinas, California 93901
(408) 757-2092

**FIREPLACE DISTRIBUTORS OF NEVADA**
120 Woodland Ave.
Reno, Nevada 89523
(702) 747-1346

**MALM FIREPLACE CENTER**
368 Yolanda Ave.
Santa Rosa, California 95404
(707) 523-7747
(707) 546-8959 (Fax)

**CANYON FIREPLACE**
2600 E. Katella Suite A
Anaheim, California 92806
(714) 288-0035
(888) 723-3347 (CA Only)

**ENERGY ALTERNATIVES**
1626 W. Pueblo Blvd.
Pueblo, Colorado 81004
(719) 564-9444

**WESTERN FIREPLACE SUPPLY**
1315 Ford St.
Colorado Springs, Colorado 80915
(719) 591-0020

**FIREPLACE WEST**
2454 Hwy 6 & 50
Grand Junction, Colorado 81505
(970) 245-2448

**D J HANNON GAS SHOP**
1930 E Boulder
Colorado Springs, Colorado 80909
(719) 577-9488

**VILLAGE HEARTH & HOME**
462 Silas Deane Hwy
Wethersfield, Connecticut 06109
(860) 249-1212

**NOVICKY INCORPORATED**
75 Grays Bridge Rd.
Brookfield, Connecticut 06804
(203) 775-2367

**FIREPLACES & STOVES BY SUPERIOR**
1457 Meriden Waterbury Rd.
Milldale, Connecticut 06467
(860) 620-5555
(888) 966-3427

**HOME HEARTH & PATIO**
428 W. Putnam Ave.
Greenwich, Connecticut 06830
(203) 622-4699

**SHELTON WINAIR CO.**
740 River Rd.
Shelton, Connecticut 06484
(203) 929-6319

**AFTERGLOW ENERGY CENTER**
1592 N. Broad St.
Jct 5 & 15 Berlin Turnpike
Meriden, Connecticut 06450
(203) 235-0033
(800) 222-4340 (CT Only)
afterglow@snet.net

**COMFORT ONE**
990 Baltimore Pike
Glen Mills, Pennsylvania 19331
(610) 459-4665

**HEARTH & HOME**
7811 Black Beach Rd.
Panama City Beach, Florida 32407
(904) 235-9099

**A PLUS FIREPLACES**
8133 Ridge Rd.
Port Richey, Florida 34668
(813) 847-6248
(800) 282-1117

**HOLMES LUMBER CO.**
6550 Roosevelt Blvd.
Jacksonville, Florida 32244
(904) 772-6100

**RESIDENTIAL CONSTRUCTION SPECIALTIES**
1716 Premier Row
Orlando, Florida 32809
(407) 859-0080

**RESIDENTIAL CONSTRUCTION SPECIALTIES**
6582 Peachtree Industrial Blvd.
Norcross, Georgia 30091
(770) 368-0646
(800) 542-7407

**RESIDENTIAL CONSTRUCTION SPECIALTIES**
400 N. Glynn St.
Fayetteville, Georgia 30214
(770) 461-2500

**RESIDENTIAL CONSTRUCTION SPECIALTIES**
2996 Canton Rd.
Marietta, Georgia 30066
(770) 426-0808
(770) 426-1108 (Fax)

**RESIDENTIAL CONSTRUCTION SPECIALTIES**
593 Sigman Rd.
Conyers, Georgia 30013
(770) 929-3412
(770) 929-1736 (Fax)

**HEARTH & PATIO SHOP**
2316 Main St.
Tucker, Georgia 30084
(770) 934-8646

**CHEROKEE STOVE BARN**
2232 Lumpkin Rd.
Augusta, Georgia 30906
(706) 790-1184
(800) 832-8565

**HEARTH OF GOLD, INC.**
110 Washington St.
Gainesville, Georgia 30501
(770) 536-6299
(800) 433-4328

**AMERICAN SPECIALTIES CO., INC.**
4408 Columbus Rd.
Macon, Georgia 31206
(912) 474-0074
(912) 474-1349 (Fax)

**COWETA POOL & FIREPLACE**
161-B Temple Ave.
Newnan, Georgia 30263
(770) 253-9492

**HOUSTON SPECIALTY SUPPLY**
107 S. Corder Rd.
Warner Robins, Georgia 31088
(912) 922-9974

**ALLIED LP GAS CO.**
331 S. Houston Lake Rd.
Warner Robins, Georgia 31088
(912) 953-3900
(800) 292-6665 (GA only)

**MODERN GAS CO. INC.**
507 W. Broad Ave.
Albany, Georgia 31707
(912) 435-6116

**THE FIREPLACE CENTER**
256 Kamehameha Ave.
Hilo, Hawaii 96720-2836
(808) 961-5646
(808) 961-5623 (Fax)
(800) 760-5646

**THRIFTWAY STOVE & FIREPLACE SHOP**
3300 Chinden
Boise, Idaho 83714
(208) 344-6592

**QUALITY STOVES**
100 W. Prairie Ave.
Burley, Idaho 83318
(208) 772-9111

**L.G.D. FIREPLACE SALES**
5840 N. Government Way
Coeur D'Alene, Idaho 83814
(208) 772-1800

**MIKES HEATING**
3504 9th St.
Lewiston, Idaho 83501
(208) 743-0776
(208) 746-3815 (Fax)

**BARNETT MAJESTIC**
1620 5th Ave.
Moline, Illinois 61265
(309) 762-8030

**COLLINS FIREPLACE**
561 Dundee Rd.
Wheeling, Illinois 60090
(847) 541-4780

**K.B.L., INC.**
4700 Brandywine Dr.
Peoria, Illinois 61614
(309) 685-9753

**SOUTHWEST FIREPLACES**
11921 S. 80th Ave.
Palos Park, Illinois 60464
(708) 448-3883

**HOUSE OF FIREPLACES**
824 E. Chicago St.
Elgin, Illinois 60120
(847) 741-6464

**FIREPLACE IN SHOPPE**
7201 Kingery
Willowbrook, Illinois 60521
(630) 323-8136

**GRASS ROOTS ENERGY INC.**
28751 N. Rand Rd. Rt. 12
Wauconda, Illinois 60084
(847) 526-5888

**LITE BRITE DIST.**
475 E. Broadway
Trenton, Illinois 62293
(618) 224-7314

**ELGIN MAJESTIC**
824 East Chicago St.
Elgin, Illinois 60120
(847) 741-5903

**ANSELMO'S**
1235 W. LeFevre Rd.
Sterling, Illinois 61081
(815) 625-3519
(815) 625-8557 (Fax)

**CLAYTON SALES**
815 East Eldorado St.
Decatur, Illinois 62521
(217) 428-4151
(800) 252-1606 (IL Only)

**ALL TEMP FIREPLACE**
112 W. Lake
Bloomingdale, Illinois 60108
(630) 893-4112

**FIREPLACE IN SHOPPE**
3348 Ridge Rd.
Lansing, Illinois 60438
(708) 895-3323

**PETERS HEATING & AIR CONDITIONING**
4520 Broadway
Quincy, Illinois 62301
(217) 222-1368

**FIREPLACE PLACE**
643 S. Rt. 59
Aurora, Illinois 60504
(630) 851-9800
(603) 851-9860 (Fax)

**NORDINES**
1601 S. Bunn St.
Bloomington, Illinois 61701
(309) 828-6054

**HEARTH & HOME**
530 W. Northwest Hwy
Mt. Prospect, Illinois 60056
(847) 259-7550
(847) 259-7570 (Fax)

**WATSEKA BOTTLE GAS**
113 N. Third
Watseka, Illinois 60970
(815) 432-4941

**MAZE LUMBER**
1100 Water St.
Peru, Illinois 61354
(815) 223-1742

**HOUSE OF FIREPLACES**
7226 E. 87th St.
Indianapolis, Indiana 46256
(317) 577-0400
(800) 677-0401

**STONE WALL MASONRY, INC.**
1235 W. Hively
Elkhart, Indiana 46517
(219) 522-5200

**FIREPLACE & GAS CENTER**
6442 Pendleton Ave.
Anderson, Indiana 46013
(317) 642-9946

**DUNCAN'S FIREPLACE & PATIO CENTER**
3837 High School Rd.
Indianapolis, Indiana 46254
(317) 299-2229
(317) 299-0848 (Fax)

**B & V DISTRIBUTING INC.**
1802 Spencer Ave.
Marion, Indiana 46952
(765) 662-0445
(765) 668-7094

**DAVIDSON-WILSON GREENHOUSES, INC.**
Rt. 2 Box 168 Ladoga Rd.
Crawfordsville, Indiana 47933
(317) 364-0556

**FIREPLACE DISTRIBUTORS OF INDIANA**
1385 S 10th St.
Noblesville, Indiana 46060
(317) 776-9445
(317) 776-9919

**STEINHARDT ENTERPRISES, INC.**
228 West LaGrange Rd.
Hanover, Indiana 47243
(812) 866-2400
(812) 866-2424

**HOME & HEARTH HEADQUARTERS**
5954 Stellhorn Rd.
Fort Wayne, Indiana 46815
(219) 485-3768

*Dealers in Indiana –Michigan*

**BASSEMIERS**
4220 E. Morgan Ave.
Evansville, Indiana 47715
(812) 479-6338

**HOOSIER HEARTH DIST.**
613 N. Madison St.
Muncie, Indiana 47305
(317) 289-0681

**WARSAW MASONRY SUPPLY**
1403 N. Detroit.
Warsaw, Indiana 46580
(219) 267-2825

**RALSTON CREEK**
2301 Hwy 6 West
Coralville, Iowa 52241
(319) 351-4780

**WOODBURNING STOVE SHOP**
10457 Hickman Rd.
Des Moines, Iowa 50322
(515) 270-5377

**DUBUQUE FIREPLACE & PATIO**
925 Century Dr.
Dubuque, Iowa 52002
(319) 582-5156

**FIRESIDE CORNER, INC.**
2700 N. Fairview Ave.
Roseville, Minnesota 55113
(612) 633-1042
(800) 541-5414

**FIREPLACE PROFESSIONALS**
1217 W. 41st St.
Sioux Falls, South Dakota 57105
(605) 339-0775
(800) 366-4328

**DIXSON'S FLOORS & MORE**
Rt. 4 Hwy 34 W.
Ottumwa, Iowa 52501
(515) 684-5093

**RALSTON CREEK**
1095 N. Center Point Rd.
Hiawatha, Iowa 52233
(319) 393-3838

**KANSAS BUILDING SUPPLY**
707 South Washington
Wichita, Kansas 67211
(316) 269-0481

**KANSAS CITY BUILDING SUPPLY**
7600 Wedd
Overland Park, Kansas 66204
(913) 962-5227

**MIDWEST FIREPLACE**
529 N. Lindenwood
Olathe, Kansas 66062
(913) 764-5575

**FIREPLACE DISTRIBUTORS INC.**
5810 Fern Valley Rd.
Louisville, Kentucky 40228
(502) 964-5996

**FIREPLACE DISTRIBUTORS OF THE BLUE GRASS**
125-A Trade St.
Lexington, Kentucky 40510
(606) 233-1039

**FIREPLACE DISTRIBUTORS OF NORTHERN KENTUCKY**
10135 Dixie Hwy
Florence, Kentucky 41042
(606) 746-3473

**NEW ENGLAND HEARTH & PATIO**
8141 Mall Rd.
Florence, Kentucky 41042
(606) 282-7272

Currently there are no Authorized Dealers listed in the state of Louisiana. Please consult a state near you or contact Heat-N-Glo at 1-888-743-2887 for additional dealers in your vicinity.

**BLACK STOVE SHOP**
49 U.S. Route 1
Yarmouth, Maine 04096
(207) 846-9030

**SUNRISE HOME & HEARTH**
Bar Harbor Rd.
Ellsworth, Maine 04605
(207) 667-3206

**THE FINEST KIND**
9 Commercial St.
Portland, Maine 04101
(207) 772-2155
(207) 772-5172 (Fax)

**THE FIREPLACE SHOP**
16165 Shady Grove Rd.
Gaithersburg, Maryland 20877
(301) 990-7272
(800) 834-8657 (MD Only)

**WARNER'S INC.**
1201 Virginia Ave.
Cumberland, Maryland 21502
(301) 724-0774
(301) 724-0790 (Fax)

**CHELMSFORD FIREPLACE**
73 Summer St.
Chelmsford, Massachusetts 01824
(508) 256-6328

**WOODSTOVES & FIREPLACES UNLIMITED**
193 E. Grove St.
Middleboro, Massachusetts 02346
(508) 947-8835

**SPA KING FACTORY OUTLET**
848 Southbridge St.
Auburn, Massachusetts 01501
(508) 832-8827
(800) 662-7727

**YANKEE FIREPLACE & GRILL CITY**
140 S. Main St.
Middleton, Massachusetts 01949
(978) 774-2760

**ROSE FORGE**
320 Underpass Rd.
Brewster, Massachusetts 02631
(508) 896-6505

**FIRESIDE DESIGN**
1458 Riverdale St.
West Springfield, Massachusetts 01089
(413) 733-0910

**IRON HOUSE**
95 Corporation St.
Hyannis, Massachusetts 02610
(508) 771-4799

**OLDE HADLEIGH HEARTH & HOME**
119 Williamansett St.
South Hadley, Massachusetts 01075
(413) 538-9845

**ENERGY UNLIMITED OF NE INC.**
303 Boston Post Rd.
Wayland, Massachusetts 01778
(508) 358-7358

**FEENS COUNTRY LIVING**
975 Merriam Ave.
Twin City Mall
Leominster, Massachusetts 01456
(508) 537-4518

**STOVE DEPOT**
1049 Turnpike St.
Canton, Massachusetts 02021
(617) 821-0777

**CHIMNEY SPECIALIST**
2158 Old 27 S.
Gaylord, Michigan 49735
(517) 732-1116
(800) 797-7710

**FIRESIDE DESIGN INC.**
921 W. Savidge St. M-104
Spring Lake, Michigan 49456
(616) 846-3666
(800) 396-9100

**FIREPLACE & SPA BUILDER DIVISION**
12555 Belden Court
Livonia, Michigan 48150
(313) 513-0461
(800) 433-0391

**FIREPLACE & SPA CLEARANCE CENTER**
35400 Plymouth Road
Livonia, MI 48150
(313) 525-7727

**EMMETTS ENERGY**
70790 Van Dyke
Romeo, Michigan 48065
(810) 752-2075

**STOREY STONE**
3904 Francis St.
Jackson, Michigan 49203
(517) 782-4033

**THE BELLOWS**
3983 E. Wilder
Bay City MI 48706
(517) 686-7070

**THE BELLOWS**
3260 Bay Rd.
Saginaw, Michigan 48603
(517) 792-3333

**POSITIVE CHIMNEY & FIREPLACE**
6717 E. M-115
Cadillac, Michigan 49601
(616) 775-7941

**MODERN HARDWARE**
1500 Kalamazoo Ave. SE
Grand Rapids, Michigan 49507
(616) 241-2655

**PHILLIPS ENERGY**
989 S. Airport Rd. W
Traverse City, Michigan 49684
(616) 929-1396

**FIREPLACE & SPA**
42647 Ford Rd.
Canton, Michigan 48185
(313) 981-4700

**FIREPLACE & SPA**
23600 Telegraph
Southfield, Michigan 48034
(810) 353-0001

**FIREPLACE & SPA**
45490 Utica Park Blvd.
Utica, Michigan 48317
(810) 726-7100

**HEARTHCREST**
2176 Wealthy St. SE
Grand Rapids, Michigan 49506
(616) 456-5300

**FIRESIDE & HEARTH SUPPLY CO.**
349 McCormick Dr.
Lapeer, Michigan 48446
(810) 667-4466

**HOT STUFF FOR PLAY, FIREPLACE & SPA INC.**
1025 S. Mission
Mt. Pleasant, Michigan 48858
(517) 772-1195

**NORTHWEST SHOOTERS SUPPLY**
4766 Holton Rd.
Twin Lake, MI 49457
(616) 828-6894

**RAMSEYER'S HEARTH N HOME**
3524 N East St.
Lansing, Michigan 48906
(517) 482-2033

**PHILLIPS ENERGY**
2309 US 31 N.
Petoskey, Michigan 49770
(616) 347-8720

**HEARTH-N-HOME, INC.**
4725 E. Houghton Lake Dr.
Houghton Lake, Michigan 48629
(517) 366-4403
(800) 799-7648

**THE FIREPLACE SHOP**
13233 West Michigan Ave.
Marshall, Michigan 49068
(616) 781-4064
(616) 781-4576 (Fax)

**BLUEWATER HEARTH & HOME**
1439 Pine Grove Ave.
Port Huron, Michigan 48060
(810) 987-3627

**AQUAMIST/FIRESIDE SHOPPE**
18701 Northline.
Southgate, Michigan 48195
(313) 287-4545

**ROYAL FIREPLACE**
6611 Center Industrial Dr.
Jenison, Michigan 49428
(616) 669-9090

**DAN'S POWER & STOVE**
6509 Main St.
Cass City, Michigan 48726
(517) 872-3190
(517) 872-4069 (Fax)

**MR. FIREPLACE**
5060 Jackson Rd.
Ann Arbor, Michigan 48103
(313) 213-2737

**LAKE SHORE CEMENT PRODUCTS**
5251 N. US 23
Oscoda, Michigan 48750
(517) 739-9341
(517) 739-0652 (Fax)

**A-1 MECHANICAL**
615 S. Waverly Rd.
Lansing, Michigan 48917
(517) 321-5631
(517) 321-3161 (Fax)

**GREAT LAKES ENERGY SYSTEMS**
1930 N. Lincoln Rd.
Escanaba, Michigan 49829
(906) 789-9616

**HEAT-N-SWEEP**
6468 E. Atherton Rd.
Burton, Michigan 48519
(810) 743-7776
(810) 743-0751

**HEAT-N-SWEEP**
2041 West Grand River
Okemos, Michigan 48864
(517) 349-2555

**FIREPLACE NORTH**
121 Kent St.
Iron Mountain, MI 49801
(906) 774-20211
(800) 974-2021

**FIRESIDE CORNER**
3850 W. Highway 13
Burnsville, Minnesota 55337
(612) 890-0758

**FIRESIDE CORNER, INC.**
2700 N. Fairview Ave.
Roseville, Minnesota 55113
(612) 633-1042
(800) 541-5414

**ACE HARDWARE DOWNTOWN**
212 W. Superior St.
Duluth, Minnesota 55802
(218) 722-4496

**HILL'S PLUMBING & HEATING**
3801 Bemidji Ave N.
Bemidji, Minnesota 56601
(218) 751-1286

**FIRESIDE CORNER**
1420 N. Riverfront St.
Mankato, Minnesota 56001
(507) 345-8084

**FIREPLACE PROFESSIONALS**
1217 W. 41st St.
Sioux Falls, South Dakota 57105
(605) 339-0775
(800) 366-4328

**FERGUS FALLS BRICK & SUPPLY**
404 S. Burlington Ave.
Fergus Falls, Minnesota 56537
(218) 739-3671

**DJ'S FIREPLACE SHOWROOM**
6060 Labeaux Ave.
Albertville, Minnesota 55301
(612) 497-4211

**DJ'S FIREPLACE SHOWROOM**
9940 Hwy. 10
Elk River, Minnesota 55330
(612) 421-5313

**TOTAL COMFORT SYSTEMS**
300 Downtown Plaza
Fairmont, Minnesota 56031
(507) 235-5278

**HUTCHINSON FIREPLACE**
218 S. Main St.
Hutchinson, Minnesota 55350
(320) 587-2164

**FIRESIDE CORNER**
225 Cty. Rd. 81
Osseo, Minnesota 55369
(612) 425-9656

**NORTHLAND BRICK & FIREPLACE**
501 Evergreen Dr. S.
Brainerd, Minnesota 56401
(218) 829-1929

**FIRESIDE CORNER**
1001 E. Hwy 12
Wilmar, Minnesota 56201
(320) 235-7415

**ENERGY PRODUCTS**
497 37th St. NE
Rochester, Minnesota 55906-3401
(507) 289-7496

**FIRESIDE CORNER**
109 4th St. NE
Waite Park, Minnesota 56387
(320) 251-2717
(800) 544-8247
(320) 251-2877 (Fax)

**CONDOR FIREPLACE & STONE CO.**
8282 Arthur St. NE
Spring Lake Park, Minnesota 55432
(612) 786-2341
(612) 786-7276 (Fax)

**THE FIREPLACE STORE**
2510 Broadway St. South
Alexandria, Minnesota 56308
(320) 762-8645
(320) 762-8054 (Fax)

**FIREPLACE CONNECTION**
140 26th St. NW
Owatonna, Minnesota 55060
(507) 444-0067
(507) 444-9707 (Fax)

**COUNTRYSIDE HEATING & COOLING**
6511 Hwy 12
Maple Plain, Minnesota 55359
(612) 479-1600
(612) 479-2518 (Fax)

**GREENMAN HEATING & REFRIDGERATION INC.**
1001 4th St. SE
Austin, Minnesota 55912
(507) 437-6500
(507) 433-8781 (Fax)

**TRUE VALUE HOME CENTER**
Hwy 59 N. Box 831
Marshall, Minnesota 56258
(507) 532-3296

*Dealers in Mississippi – New York*

**BMC SALES**
2669 Highway 45 South.
P.O. Box 1351
Saltillo, Mississippi 38866
(601) 869-2619

**BMC SALES, INC. #2**
7060 Ashley Cove
Olive Branch, Mississippi 38654
(601) 895-2431

**BOLIVAR INSULATION**
1601 W. 4th
Joplin, Missouri 64801
(417) 623-2530

**THE ALTERNATIVE GRILL & FIRESIDE SHOPPE**
177 Concord Plaza
St. Louis, Missouri 63128
(314) 849-0077

**THE ALTERNATIVE GRILL & FIRESIDE SHOPPE**
15053 Manchester Rd.
Ballwin, Missouri 63011
(314) 256-6564

**BOLIVAR INSULATION**
South Bus. Hwy 13
Bolivar, Missouri 65613
(417) 326-7668

**THE ALTERNATIVE GRILL & FIRESIDE SHOPPE**
2661 Metro Blvd.
Maryland Heights, Missouri 63043
(314) 291-5300

**BOLIVAR INSULATION**
2050 E. Trafficway
Springfield, Missouri 65801
(417) 862-5575

**COMFORT HEATING**
1923 N. Woodbine
St. Joseph, Missouri 64506
(816) 364-6540

**CLEMENS POOL & SPA**
Rt. 4 Box 140
Marshall, Missouri 65340
(816) 886-7613

**MIDWEST FIREPLACE**
529 N. Lindenwood
Olathe, Kansas 66062
(913) 764-5575

**STAR HEATING & AIR CONDITIONING**
1702 Commerce Ct.
Columbia, Missouri 65202
(573) 449-3784

**R. BOGG STEEL & STOVE**
3518 N. Ten Mile Dr.
Jefferson City, Missouri 65109
(573) 893-2525

**BUSCH FURNITURE**
12345 Hwy 63 S.
Rolla, Missouri 65401
(573) 364-3448
(573) 364-8022

**PICKS FIREPLACES PLUS**
Hwy 42 South, Box 165
Kaiser, Missouri 65047
(573) 348-9100
(573) 348-9200 (Fax)

**OUTDOOR POWER EQUIPMENT & FIREPLACE CENTER**
510 S. 4th St.
St. Genevieve, Missouri 63670
(573) 883-2845
(888) 883-2845
(573) 883-9959 (Fax)

**HACKMANN LUMBER**
2601 Hwy K
O'Fallon, Missouri 63366
(314) 240-8360
(314) 240-8362 (Fax)

**HARRIS HEATING & COOLING**
415 W. Karsch Blvd
Farmington, Missouri 63640-0737
(573) 756-4297
(573) 756-7559 (Fax)

**SERVICE EXPRESS**
310 N. Main St.
Kirksville, Missouri 63501
(816) 665-8752

**NEW HAMPTON HARDWARE**
206 E. Lincoln St. Box 287
New Hampton, Missouri 64471
(660) 439-3245

**GINNATY HEATING**
1425 18th Ave. S.
Great Falls, Montana 59405
(406) 452-7665

**LUMBERMEN'S**
13709 Industrial Rd.
Omaha, Nebraska 68137
(402) 894-2222

**CAPITAL PATIO/THE FLAME SHOP**
5500 Old Cheney Rd. Ste.16
Lincoln, Nebraska 68516
(402) 421-7575

**NATIONAL INSULATION HEARTH & HOME**
1701 Cushman Dr. #6
Lincoln, Nebraska 68512
(402) 421-8070

**APEX STOVES, INC.**
288 E. Winnie Ln.
Carson City, Nevada 89706
(702) 883-2102
(702) 883-7512 (Fax)

**FIREPLACE DISTRIBUTORS OF NEVADA**
120-A Woodland Ave.
Reno, Nevada 89523
(702) 747-1346
(702) 747-1387 (Fax)

**THE COUNTRY LIVING CENTER**
114 Lafayette Rd.
Hampton Falls, New Hampshire 03844
(603) 926-2424
(603) 926-2424 (Fax)

**NORDIC STOVE SHOP**
75 Dover Point Rd.
Dover, New Hampshire 03820
(603) 749-4660

**ESERSKY'S HARDWARD**
46 Union St.
Claremont, New Hampshire 03743
(603) 542-6031
(603) 543-9522 (Fax)

**FYRESIDE N.J.**
911 First Avenue
Asbury Park, New Jersey 07712
(732) 776-7200
(732) 776-7207 (fax)

**STAR DISTRIBUTORS**
1512 South Black Horse Pike
Williamstown, New Jersey 08094
(609) 728-4444
(800) 992-0720

**BRIGHT ACRES**
Hwy. 34 at Allaire Rd.
Wall Township, New Jersey 07719
(908) 974-0110

**D & W CHIMNEY**
95 Route 22 Eastbound
White House Station, New Jersey 08889
(908) 534-9701

**J B FIREPLACES, INC.**
875 Rt. 17 South
Airmont Ave.
Ramsey, New Jersey 07446
(201) 760-9585

**GOLDEN FLAME DISTRIBUTING, INC.**
Call for Additional Dealers
15855 N. Greenway-Hayden Loop
Suite 170
Scottsdale, Arizona 85260
(602) 948-9919
(800) 820-2373

**CENTRAL FIREPLACE**
5525 Transit Rd.
Williamsville, New York 14221
(716) 636-9753

**HAMBURG FIREPLACE**
4670 Camp Rd.
Hamburg, New York 14075
(716) 649-3473

**FIREPLACE FASHIONS**
1936 Hudson Ave.
Rochester, New York 14617
(716) 266-8967

**ACE SWIM & LEISURE**
3313 Chili Ave.
Rochester, New York 14624
(716) 889-2310

**HEARTHS A FIRE**
RR 2 Box 2063 RT 23
Oneonta, New York 13820
(607) 436-9549

**AMERICAN STOVE**
5891 Firestone Dr.
Syracuse, New York 13206
(315) 433-0038

**AMERICAN FIREPLACE & GIFT**
728 Broad St.
Utica, New York 13501
(315) 732-4158

**SUNDANCE LEISURE**
19281 US Rte 11
Watertown, New York 13601
(315) 788-2207

**CORNING NATURAL GAS**
1100 Clemens Pkwy
Elmira, New York 14901
(607) 733-4328

*Dealers in New York – Oregon*

**CORNING NATURAL GAS**
330 W. William St.
Corning, New York 14830
(607) 936-3755

**BEST FIRE**
1760 Central Ave.
Albany, New York 12205
(518) 869-9600
(518) 869-1931 (Fax)

**SARATOGA MASONRY**
Rt 9 Maple Ave.
Saratoga Springs, New York 12866
(518) 587-6300
sms-sfg@worldnet.att.net

**THE FIREPLACE & PATIO SHOPPE**
369 White Plains Post Rd.
Eastchester, New York 10709
(914) 337-5301

**FIREPLACES OF LONG ISLAND/PICONE ENERGY, INC.**
180 Long Island Ave.
Holtsville, New York 11742
(516) 289-5490

**THE FIREPLACE STORE**
(Div. of COAL RITE CORP)
3540 Merrick Rd.
Seaford, New York 11783
(516) 785-0047

**ALL SEASONS GALLERY**
119 Rocky Point Rd.
Middle Island, New York 11953
(516) 924-0738

**BASIC ENERGY**
500 Jericho Turnpike
Mineola, New York 11501
(516) 294-9044

**BASIC ENERGY EAST**
716 East Jericho Turnpike
Huntington Station, New York 11746
(516)547-5100

**FIRE GLOW**
1565 Richmond Rd.
Staten Island, New York 10304
(718) 979-9191

**PARNELL POOLS**
1573 Roberts Ave.
Lumberton, North Carolina 28358
(910) 738-8110

**SUNRISE APPLIANCE CENTER**
2444 Hwy 70 S.E.
Hickory, North Carolina 28602
(704) 327-9947

**CHIMNEY MASTERS**
Rt 6 Box 120/Gibson Rd.
Hertford, North Carolina 27944
(919) 264-4420

**KITCHEN DESIGN BY COX**
742 N. Broad St.
Mooresville, North Carolina 28115
(704) 663-0156

**CORONADO PRODUCTS**
3709 Memorial Hwy
P.O. Box 1045
Mandan, North Dakota 58554
(701) 663-7902
(800) 462-4409 (ND Only)

**CORONADO PRODUCTS**
1150 3rd Ave. W
Dickinson, North Dakota 58601
(701) 227-8441
(701) 227-3610 (Fax)

**DAYTON FIREPLACE SYSTEMS INC.**
450 Gargrave Rd.
West Carrollton, Ohio 45449
(937) 847-8139
(937) 847-8461 (FAX)

**DEHAVEN HOME & GARDEN**
15276 US 224 East
Findlay, Ohio 45840
(419) 422-5617

**DEHAVEN HOME & GARDEN**
775 Shawnee Rd.
Lima, Ohio 45805
(419) 227-7003

**READING ROCK**
4600 Devitt Drive
Cincinnati, Ohio 45246
(513) 874-2345

**BUSH'S QUALITY FIREPLACE**
11216 Gladstone Rd.
Warren, Ohio 44481
(330) 538-2367

**KERNS FIREPLACE & HEATER SALES**
5217 Tama Rd.
Celina, Ohio 45822
(419) 363-2230

**THE WOODBURNERS**
6715 N. Ridge Rd.
Madison, Ohio 44057
(216) 428-6434

**PARADISE COVE**
1220 West Wooster
Bowling Green, Ohio 43402
(419) 352-7776

**CUSTOM FIREPLACE**
5537 Whipple Ave. NW
N. Canton, Ohio 44720
(330) 499-7341

**ROBERT'S SPECIALTY**
505-521 E. Perkins Ave.
Sandusky, Ohio 44870
(419) 626-3178

**COUNTRY STOVE**
6669 Royalton Rd.
N. Royalton, Ohio 44133
(216) 582-0062

**THE FIREPLACE**
2377 State Rte 18
Medina, Ohio 44256
(330) 239-4000

**COLONIAL FIREPLACES**
449 Powell Rd.
State Route 750
Powell, Ohio 43065
(614) 764-0320

**JENNINGS HEATING**
1671 E. Market St.
Akron, Ohio 44305
(330) 784-1286

**SUBURBAN FIREPLACE**
820 Refugee Rd.
Pickerington, Ohio 43147
(614) 864-5604

**HEAT EXCHANGE**
34205 Lorain Rd.
N. Ridgeville, Ohio 44039
(216) 327-6242

**ASHLAND COMFORT CONTROL**
805 E. Main
Ashland, Ohio 44805
(419) 281-0144

**NORTH CENTRAL INSULATION**
7539 St. Rt. 13 South
Belleville, Ohio 44813
(419) 886-2030

**THE FIRESIDE SHOP**
1232 Brandywine Blvd.
Zanesville, Ohio 43701
(614) 450-7480

**PARADISE COVE**
26580 N. Dixie Hwy Suite 107
Perrysburg, Ohio 43551
(419) 874-6622
(419) 874-6668 (Fax)

**COMFORTEC**
13221 Lincoln Way West
Massillon, Ohio 44647
(330) 832-6444

Currently there are no Authorized Dealers listed in the state of Oklahoma. Please consult a state near you or contact Heat-N-Glo at 1-888-743-2887 for additional dealers in your vicinity.

**MOUNTAIN VIEW HEATING**
480 SE Bridgeford Blvd.
Bend, Oregon 97702
(541) 389-6714

**ANCHOR FIREPLACE PRODUCTS**
14175 SW Galbreath Dr.
Sherwood, Oregon 97140
(503) 925-8888

**ROTH HEATING**
593 SE. 1st Ave.
Canby, Oregon 97013
(503) 266-1249

**MARSHALL'S HEATING**
4110 Olympic St.
Springfield, Oregon 97478
(541) 747-7445

**ORLEY'S STOVE & SPA CENTER**
3050 Crater Lake Hwy.
Medford, Oregon 97504
(541) 779-5340

**FIREPLACE SHOWCASE**
1601 SE River Rd.
Hillsboro, Oregon 97123
(503) 640-3607

**HOME FIRE STOVE SHOPPE**
1695 Market St. NE
Salem, Oregon 97301
(503) 364-6339
1-800-656-6339 (OR Only)

**FIRESIDE DIST. OF OREGON**
18389 SW Boones Ferry Rd.
Portland, Oregon 97224
(503) 684-8535

*Dealers in Pennsylvania – Washington*

**COMFORT ONE**
990 Baltimore Pike
Glen Mills, Pennsylvania 19331
(610) 459-4665

**WOOD HEAT**
1924 Rt 212 Pleasant Valley
Quakertown, Pennsylvania 18951
(610) 346-7894
(800) 444-4328

**LUPPOLD HEATING**
Leisz's Rd & Ulrich Ln.
Leesport, Pennsylvania 19533
(610) 926-5522

**S & T COOMBE, INC.**
Rt. 940 Liberty Plaza
Pocono Lake, Pennsylvania 18347
(717) 646-8254

**SHORT'S STOVES, CHIMNEYS &
FIREPLACES**
1601 Elizabeth Ave.
Laureldale, Pennsylvania 19605
(610) 929-1813
(610) 929-3350 (Fax)

**WOODY'S FIREPLACE**
130 Narrows Rd.
Larksville, Pennsylvania 18651
(717) 283-2534
(800) 468-7855
(717) 283-2571 (Fax)

**GLICK ASSOCIATES INC.**
Rte 15 N.
Selinsgrove, Pennsylvania 17870
(717) 743-7332
(800) 262-3268

**W.L. STERNER**
516 Frederick St.
Hanover, Pennsylvania 17331
(717) 637-2159
(717) 633-5538 (Fax)

**NICKOS CHIMNEY CO.**
US Rt. 30 Box 207
Latrobe, Pennsylvania 15650
(412) 532-0070

**BUCK STOVE OF BEAVER VALLEY**
1478 Broadhead Rd.
Monaca, Pennsylvania 15061
(412) 728-2422

**HEARTH & HOME FURNISHINGS**
300 North Main St.
Zelienople, Pennsylvania 16063
(724) 452-6732

**HOWELL CRAFT INC.**
591 Simpson Howell Rd.
Elizabeth, Pennsylvania 15037
(412) 751-6861
(412) 751-0213 (Fax)

**THE FIREPLACE AND PATIO PLACE**
1651 McFarland Rd. South Hills
Pittsburgh, Pennsylvania 15216
(412) 343-5157

**THE FIREPLACE AND PATIO PLACE**
4920 McKnight Rd.
Pittsburgh, Pennsylvania 15237
(412) 366-6970
(412) 366-8046

**THE FIREPLACE AND PATIO PLACE**
4680 Old William Penn Hwy
Monroeville, Pennsylvania 15146
(412) 372-3011
(412) 372-4019 (Fax)

**STOVEPIPE FIREPLACE SHOP**
654 Warwick Ave.
Warwick, Rhode Island 02888
(401) 941-9333

Currently there are no Authorized Dealers listed in
the state of South Carolina. Please consult a state
near you or contact Heat-N-Glo at 1-888-743-2887
for additional dealers in your vicinity.

**FIREPLACE PROFESSIONALS**
1217 W. 41st St.
Sioux Falls, South Dakota 57105
(605) 339-0775
(800) 366-4328

**FARMERS PROPANE GAS COOP**
P.O. Box 315
Arlington, South Dakota 57212
(605) 983-5621

**FIREPLACE SOLUTIONS**
Po Box 99
1208 Topside Rd.
Louisville, Tennessee 37777-5505
(423) 970-2600

**GAS SYSTEMS**
3206 East Stone Dr.
Kingsport, Tennessee 37660
(423) 288-0877

**THE FIRESIDE CENTER**
1203 S. Cumberland St.
Morristown, Tennessee 37813
(423) 586-4500
(423) 586-4031 (Fax)

**PERFECTION WHOLESALE**
6742-A N. Eldridge Pkwy.
Houston, Texas 77041
(713) 937-4575

**T & F BUILDING PRODUCTS**
1129 Ave. R
Grand Prairie, Texas 75050
(972) 641-6098

**NIX DOOR & HARDWARE**
921 E. Waggonan St.
Fort Worth, Texas 76110
(817) 920-9221

**FIREPLACES INC.**
973 East 2100 South
Salt Lake City, Utah 84106
(801) 486-8492

**TETON FIREPLACE DESIGN**
903 East 9400 South
Sandy, Utah 84094
(801) 233-8500

**FIREPLACE ETC.**
560 S University Ave.
Provo, Utah 84601
(801) 375-5787

**LONE PEAK GAS & EQUIPMENT SUPPLY**
1460 N. Hwy 40
Heber City, Utah 84032
(801) 654-0684

**WESTERN LIVING**
1100 W. Hwy 40
Vernal, Utah 84078
(800) 301-0525
(801) 789-0525

**CEDAR BUILDER SUPPLY**
309 N 200 W
Cedar City, Utah 84720
(801) 586-9424

**THE FIRESIDE HOME CENTER, INC.**
914 West Sunset Blvd.
St. George, Utah 84770
(801) 673-1188

**CHIMNEY SWEEP**
1970 Shelburne Rd.
Shelburne, Vermont 05482
(802) 985-4900

**PROCTOR GAS INC.**
2 Market St.
Proctor, Vermont 05765
(802) 459-3340
(802) 459-2151 (Fax)

**MT. VERNON SERVICE Co.**
8120 Richmond Hwy
Alexandria, Virginia 22302
(703) 780-2300
(703) 780-2301 (Fax)

**BETTER HOMES & PRODUCTS**
Hwy. 221 Rt 1 Box 346
Lynchburg, Virginia 24502
(804) 385-4368

**THULMAN EASTERN**
530B Aberdeen Rd.
Hampton, Virginia 23661
(804) 826-9868

**HANDY'S HEATING**
1575 Memorial Hwy.
Mt. Vernon, WA 98273
(360) 428-0969

**R & R HEATING**
4019 E. Central
Spokane, Washington 99207
(509) 484-1405

**THE FIREPLACE CENTER**
Division of RON MORRIS HEATING & AIR
CONDITIONING
1922 E. Houston
Spokane, Washington 99207
(509) 487-5058

**BEST BET PLUMBING**
3130 N. Division
Spokane, Washington 99207
(509) 324-3790

**LYNDEN SHEET METAL**
8123 Guide Meridian
Lynden, Washington 98264
(360) 354-3991

**BARTONS FIREPLACE SHOP**
E. 11401 Montgomery Dr. #3
Spokane, Washington 99207
(509) 922-5000

**BEST BET PLUMBING & HEATING**
3130 N. Division
Spokane, Washington 99207
(509) 324-3790

*Dealers in Washington – British Columbia & Alberta*

**OLYMPIA FIREPLACE SUPPLY**
506 E. 4th Ave.
Olympia, Washington 98501
(360) 352-4328
(360) 352-9492 (Fax)

**CAMPBELL & BRUCE, INC.**
2828 W. Irving
Pasco, Washington 99301
(509) 545-9848

**HERITAGE HEATING**
9001 Pacific Ave.
Tacoma, Washington 98444
(253) 922-2211

**NORTHWEST GAS FIREPLACES, INC.**
11711 NE 99th St. Suite 910
Vancouver, Washington 98682
(360) 256-9256

**BASIN REFRIGERATION**
10158 Kinder Rd.
Moses Lake, Washington 98837
(509) 765-7138
(509) 765-0979 (Fax)

**TOP HAT STOVES & POOLS**
2258 Main St.
Wheeling, West Virginia 26003
(304) 233-6262

**FIRESIDE AND PATIO SHOP**
804 Cross Lanes Dr.
Cross Lanes, West Virginia 25313
(304) 776-3546

**AMERICAN HOME FIREPLACE & PATIO**
124 S. Leonard St.
West Salem, Wisconsin 54669
(608) 786-1233

**MINOCQUA INTERIORS**
7645 Hwy 51 South
Minocqua, Wisconsin 54545
(715) 356-2021

**ALLIED FIRELITE**
310 Westhill Blvd.
Appleton, Wisconsin 54914
(414) 733-4911
(800) 236-4328 (WI only)

**MARCELL'S**
1810 6th St.
Wausau, Wisconsin 54401
(715) 848-5194

**BURNING DESIRES**
16750 C West Bluemound Rd.
Brookfield, Wisconsin 53005
(414) 782-4105

**ALLIED FIRELITE**
2540 S. Hasting Way
Eau Claire, Wisconsin 54701
(715) 832-5232

**ACE HARDWARE DOWNTOWN**
212 W. Superior St.
Duluth, Minnesota 55802
(218) 722-4496

**ENERGY SAVERS**
6298 Hwy 36
Oakdale, Minnesota 55128
(612) 770-0650

**FIREPLACE SYSTEMS**
1251 Sentry Dr.
Waukesha, Wisconsin 53186
(414) 896-3774

**TOP HAT HEATING, COOLING, CHIMNEY SPECIALISTS**
401 Linn St. (Hwy 33)
Baraboo, WI 53913
(608) 356-7268
(800) 657-6959
(608) 356-7487 (Fax)

**KILMER'S FIREPLACE STORE**
823 Hammond Ave.
Rice Lake, WI 54868
(715) 234-8898
(715) 236-2097 (FAX)

**HEARTHSIDE**
1401 Elkhorn Rd. (Highway H North)
Lake Geneva, WI 53147
(414) 249-0055

**MARCELL'S OF WISCONSIN RAPIDS**
8751 Hwy 13 South
Wisconsin Rapids, WI 54494
(715) 325-6668
(715) 325-7931 (Fax)

**SNOWBELT FIREPLACE & STOVE SHOP, INC.**
286 Wilson St.
P.O. Box 99
Amherst, WI 54406
(715) 824-3982
(715) 824-5021 (Fax)

**MADISON FIREPLACE**
6709 Watts Rd.
Madison, WI 53719
(608) 276-6010
(608) 271-2593

**BUECHEL STONE CORP.**
N 4399 Hwy 175 S
Fond du Lac, WI 54937-9266
(920) 922-4790
(920) 922-5298 (Fax)

**BUECHEL STONE CORP.**
W 3639 Hwy H
Chilton, WI 53014-9643
(920) 849-9361
(920) 849-7810 (Fax)

**D & J PELLET STOVES**
3151 Nationsway
Cheyenne, Wyoming 82001
(307) 638-4543

**MR. FIREPLACE**
#702 13377 78 Ave.
Surrey, British Columbia V3W 5B9
(604) 591-2261

**COMOX FIREPLACE & PATIO**
4911 North Island Highway
Courtenay, British Columbia V9N 5Y9
(250) 338-8522

**SHEPHERDS HARDWARE LTD.**
3525 Mill St.
PO BOX 37
Armstrong, British Columbia V0E 1B0
(250) 546-3002

**ALPHA FIREPLACE CENTRE LTD.**
#2-31550 South Fraser Way
Clearbrook, British Columbia V2T 4C6
(604) 852-1212

**QUALITY STOVES & FIREPLACES**
1702 Peterson Rd.
Campbell River, British Columbia V9W 2E6
(250) 286-0051

**A.R. DYCK HEATING LTD.**
1980 Springfield Rd.
Kelowna, British Columbia J1Y 5J7
(250) 860-6556

**BEAVER LUMBER**
150 Fairview Place
Penticton, British Columbia V2A 6A5
(250) 492-4307

**PARKSVILLE FIREPLACE**
666 E. Island Hwy.
Parksville, British Columbia V9P 1T8
(604) 248-6031

**POINTWEST SERVICES, LTD.**
805 Notre Dame Dr.
Kamloops, British Columbia V9P 1T8
(604) 248-6031

**WEST COAST OIL BURNERS**
3994 4th Ave.
Port Alberni, British Columbia V9Y 7M7
(604) 723-5111

**VAGLIO FIREPLACE**
3600 East Hastings St.
Vancouver, British Columbia V5K 2A9
(604) 298-6494

**KRAUSE'S APPLIANCES**
9550 120th St.
Surrey, British Columbia V3V 4C1
(604) 585-0667

**GASLAND EQUIPMENT & FIREPLACES, INC.**
2418 King George Hwy
Surrey, British Columbia V3S 6C4
(604) 536-0535

**J.C. FIREPLACES**
8915 Young St.
Chilliwack, British Columbia V2P 4R4
(604) 793-7871

**KIRKLAND METAL SHOP, LTD.**
6162 East Boulevard
Vancouver, British Columbia V6M 3V6
(604)261-2525

**FIRESIDE PLUMBING & HEATING**
1216 Highway 97 South
Quesnel, British Columbia V2J 4E1
(250) 747-3243

**ACADIA NORTHWEST MECHANICAL INC.**
5239 Keith Ave.
Terrace, British Columbia V8G 1L2
(250) 635-7158

**MR. FIREPLACE**
5410 - 17 Ave.SE
Calgary, Alberta T2B 1M2
(403) 272-9845

**WOOD & ENERGY STORE**
11575 149 St.
Edmonton, Alberta T5M 1W9
(403) 452-4988
(403) 452-5877 (Fax)

**VAGLIO FIREPLACE CO. 1991 LTD.**
10329 58th Ave.
Edmonton, Alberta T6H 5E4
(403) 435-3521
(403) 435-3524 (Fax)

*Dealers in Saskatchewan – Ontario*

**NORTHERN FIREPLACE LTD.**
1701 Saskatchewan Ave.
Saskatoon, Saskatchewan S7L 1P7
(306) 244-2774

**NORTHERN FIREPLACE LTD.**
140 6th Ave. East
Regina, Saskatchewan S4N 5A5
(306) 781-8007

**FLAME & COMFORT**
318 Logan Ave.
Winnipeg, Manitoiba R3A 0P5
(204) 943-5263

**DON & SON BUILDING SUPPLIES LTD.**
1289 Somerville St. N.
Oshawa, Ontario L1G 7L5
(905) 576-1765

**UNIVERSAL HVAC SYSTEMS**
1423 Upper Ottawa Unit 8
Hamilton, Ontario L8W 3J6
(905) 574-3278

**FIRESIDE PLUS**
36 Grand River St. N.
Paris, Ontario N3L 2M2
(519) 442-7400

**CENTRAL GAS HEATING & AIR CONDITIONING**
1050 Britannia Rd. E. Units 1 & 2
Mississauga, Ontario L4W 4N9
(905) 795-8300

**BETZ CUT STONE LTD.**
3440 Davis Dr.
Newmarket, Ontario L3Y 4W1
(905) 853-1258

**HEARTH-N-HOME DISTR.**
11610 County Rd. 42
RR 2 Sandwich S.
Tecumseh, Ontario N8N 2M1
(519) 735-1213

**EVANS REFRIGERATION LTD.**
4065 Stanley Ave.
Niagara Falls, Ontario L2E 4Z1
(905) 354-4424

**FIREPLACE GALLERY**
27 Dufflaw Rd.
North York, Ontario N6A 2W2
(416) 781-5470

**INTERNATIONAL FIREPLACES**
3393 Co. Rd. 42
Windsor, Ontario N9A 6J3
(519) 972-6009

**HEARTH & MANTLE**
20 Perma Ct.
St. Catherines, Ontario L2R-7K8
(905) 687-3575

**KAWARTHA FIREPLACES**
822 Rye St.
Peterborough, Ontario K9J 6W9
(705) 741-1900

**BOB'S WOODBURNERS**
803 Memorial Ave.
Thunder Bay, Ontario P7B 3Z7
(807) 345-3453
(807) 345-3097 (Fax)
bdoucet@microage-tb.com

**ULTRA COMFORT H.V.A.C. SYSTEMS**
5015 Maingate Dr. Unit 2
Mississauga, Ontario L4W 1G4
(905) 629-3383
(905) 629-3808 (Fax)

**HEARTHLAND FIREPLACES LIMITED**
5450 Mainway Dr.
Burlington, Ontario L7L 6A4
(905) 319-0474

**THE COMFORT SHOPPE**
160 Baseline Rd. East
Bowmanville, Ontario L1C-1A2
(905) 623-2956
(905) 623-2898 (Fax)

**FINELINE GAS FIREPLACES**
28 Bridgeport Rd. E.
Waterloo, Ontario N2J 2J5
(519) 725-3055
(519) 725-9284 (Fax)

**SCOTTS FIREPLACES**
48 Talbot South
Essex, Ontario N8M 1A9
(519) 776-9930
(519) 776-9932 (Fax)

**KASTLE FIREPLACE**
8294 Durham York Line
Locust Hill, Ontario L0H 1J0
(905) 472-9432
(905) 294-7058 (Fax)

**APPLEWOOD HEATING & AIR CONDITIONING LTD.**
3525 Hawkstone Rd.
Mississauga, Ontario L5N 3L9
(905) 275-4500

**THE COMFORT SHOPPE**
160 Baseline Rd. East
Bowmanville, Ontario L1C 1A2
(905) 623-2956

**MARSH'S STOVE**
3322 Dundas St. W.
Toronto, Ontario M6P 2A4
(416) 762-4582
(800) 906-5557
(416) 762-0354 (Fax)
marshs@istar.ca

**LONDON NATURAL GAS**
4026 Meadow Brook
London, Ontario N6L 1C5
(519) 652-9474

**SMALL TOWN HEATING SERVICE**
Po Box 287
Ailsa Craig, Ontario N0M 1A0
(519) 293-3888

**ROY INCH & SONS LTD.**
878 Wellington Rd.
London, Ontario N6E 1L9
(519) 681-2450

**SOO MILL LUMBER**
539 Great Northern Rd.
Sault Ste. Marie, Ontario P6B 2A4
(705) 759-8509

**SURFSIDE GROUP**
20 Charles St.
New Market, Ontario L3Y 3V8
(905) 895-1755

*Suppliers*

**COUNTRY HEARTH & CHIMNEY**
131 Peter St.
Pt. Hope, Ontario L1A 1C5
(905) 885-7629

**MASON PLACE**
25987 Woodbine Ave. RR 2
Keswick, Ontario L4P 3E9
(905) 476-5545

**NOLL CLIMATE CONTROL**
152 Booth Rd.
North Bay, Ontario P1B 8Z4
(705) 474-0768

**POLO FIREPLACES**
190 Marycroft Rd. Unit 14
Woodbridge, Ontario L4L 5Y2
(905) 851-6834

**PROPANE MONIN**
5300 Boul Levesque
Laval, Quebec H7C 1N1
(514) 661-7783

**DISTRIBUTION GAJ**
299A Boul D'an Jou
Chateaugay, Quebec J6J 2R5
(514) 691-5636

**PROPANE METM**
1973 Boul Talbot
Chicoutini, Quebec G7H 5G4
(514) 549-1712

**LUMI AIR DORION**
100 Boul lanwood
Dorion, Quebec J7V 1X9
(514) 424-9404

*OUR THANKS TO THESE SUPPLIERS:*

**BRICKSTONE STUDIOS**
2108 South 38th St.
Lincoln, Nebraska 68506
(800) 449-6599
(402) 488-5440 (Fax)

**HEAT-N-GLO FIREPLACE PRODUCTS**
6665 W. Hwy 13
Minneapolis, MN 55378
(612) 890-8367
(612) 890-3525 (Fax)
info@heatnglo.com

**STONE MAGIC**
301 Pleasant Drive
Dallas, TX 75217
(800) 398-1199
(214) 398-1293 (FAX)

**SUPERIOR CLAY CORPORATION**
Uhrichsville, Ohio
(800) 848-6166

**SUPERIOR, THE FIREPLACE COMPANY**
4325 Artesia Ave.
Fullerton, California 92633
(714) 521-7302

**WALLY LITTLE, A LITTLE WORKSHOP**
4290 Carolyn Dr.
Las Vegas, Nevada 89103
(702) 367-6775

**WOHNERS INC.**
29 Bergen St.
Englewood, New Jersey 07631
(201) 568-7307
(201) 568-7415 (FAX)

# Notes